IN success

POWERED BY
GO Math!

INCLUDES

- Indiana Academic Standards Lessons
- Lesson Practice/Homework with Spiral Review
- STEM Activity Worksheets

Printed in the U.S.A.

ISBN 978-0-544-77890-0

3 4 5 6   1421   19 18 17 16

4500602913   A B C D E F G

Table of Contents

STEM Activities

Name ______________________

Problem Solving • Equal Groups

Essential Question How can you solve problems using the strategy *make a model*?

Learning Objective You will use the strategy *make a model* using cubes to make equal groups.

Unlock the Problem Real World

DIRECTIONS Make this cube train. Break it apart into two equal trains. Draw your trains. Tell a friend about the two trains.

Try Another Problem

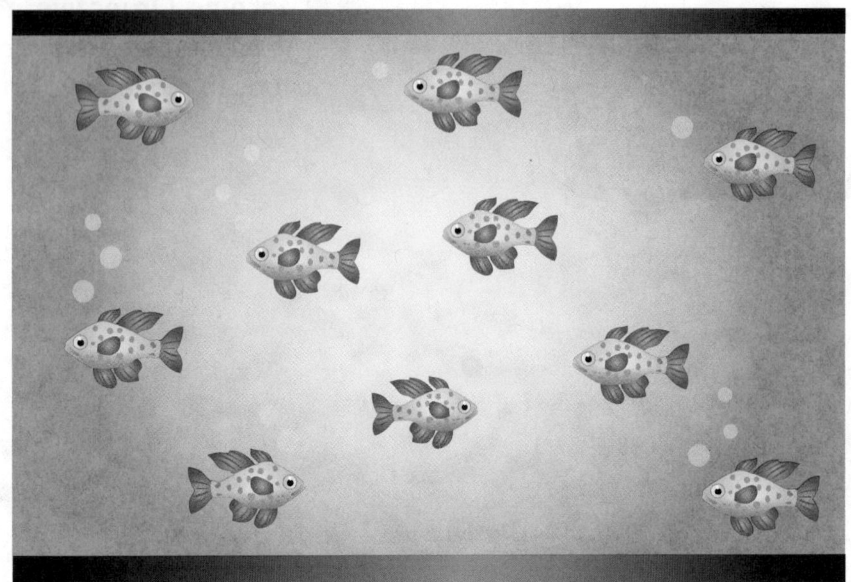

DIRECTIONS Maria wants to put the fish into 2 equal groups. How many fish will be in each bowl? Use cubes to solve the problem. **1.** Count the fish. Write how many. **2.** Put an equal number of cubes in each bowl. Write how many.

Name ______________________________

Share and Show

DIRECTIONS Use cubes to model the problem. Draw and color the groups. Write how many. **3.** Mr. Patel puts four beach chairs in two equal groups. How many chairs are in each group? **4.** Michael put eight beach balls in two equal groups. How many beach balls are in each group?

On Your Own Real World

5

WRITE Math

6

DIRECTIONS Use cubes to model and then draw to solve each problem. **5.** Mom packs 6 water bottles in equal groups in two coolers. How many water bottles are in each cooler? **6.** Grandma has more than 7 apples, but fewer than 9 apples. She packs an equal number of apples in two bags. How many apples does she put in each bag?

Name ____________________

Problem Solving • Equal Groups

Learning Objective You will use the strategy *make a model* using cubes to make equal groups.

1

2

DIRECTIONS Use cubes to model. Draw and color the groups. Write how many. **1.** Sofia put two shovels in two pails in equal groups. How many shovels are in each pail? **2.** Pedro put ten sand toys in two bags in equal groups. How many toys are in each bag?

Lesson Check

Spiral Review

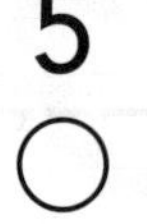

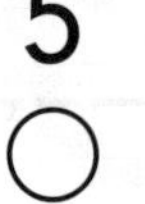

4 ○ 5 ○ 6 ○ 7 ○

DIRECTIONS 1. Max puts eight towels in two beach bags in equal groups. How many towels are in each bag? Use cubes to model. Draw and color the groups. Write how many. **2.** Ana puts four shells in two pails in equal groups. How many shells are in each pail? Use cubes to model. Draw and color the groups. Write how many. **3.** Count. Choose the correct number. **4.** Count. Write how many.

Name ________________________

One More and One Less

Essential Question How can you find a number that is one more than or one less than another number?

Learning Objective You will find one more and one less than a number.

Listen and Draw Real World

______ 8 ______

DIRECTIONS Place 8 counters in the ten frame. Take one counter away. Write the number that is one less than 8. Place 8 counters in the ten frame again. Add one more counter. Write the number that is one more than 8.

Share and Show

1

6

2

3

DIRECTIONS 1. There are 6 erasers in the set. Write the number that is one less than 6. Write the number that is one more than 6. **2.** There are 3 crayons in the set. Write the number that is one less than 3. **3.** Write the number that is one more than 3.

Name ________________________________

9

4

2

5

4

DIRECTIONS 3–5. Look at the number. Write the number that is one less. Write the number that is one more.

Problem Solving • Applications Real World

WRITE Math

6

7

DIRECTIONS 6. Gabe has 5 hats. Chloe has one more hat than Gabe. How many hats does Chloe have? Draw Chloe's hats. Write the number. 7. Jack has 3 marbles. Pat has one more marble than Jack. Draw Pat's marbles and write how many.

HOME ACTIVITY • Show your child a set of seven household objects. Have your child create a set of objects that has one more object than your set.

Name ______________________________

One More and One Less

Learning Objective You will find one more and one less than a number.

DIRECTIONS 1. There are 7 pencils in the set. Write the number that is one less than 7. Write the number that is one more than 7. **2–3.** Look at the number. Write the number that is one less. Write the number that is one more.

Lesson Check

Spiral Review

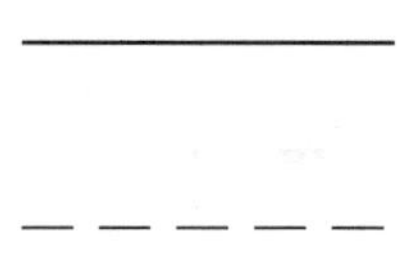

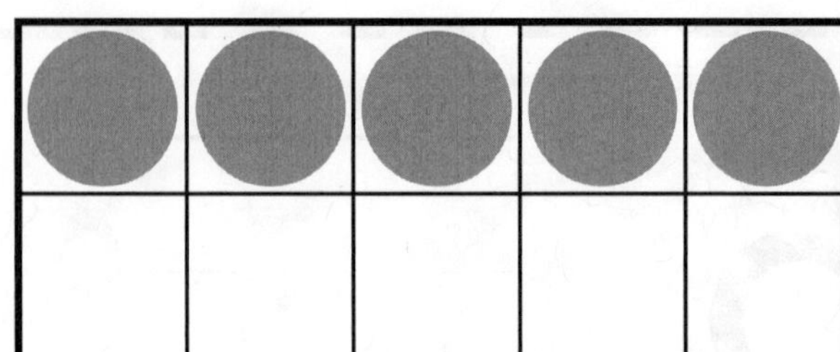

DIRECTIONS 1. Jessica has a sticker with 4 stars. Which sticker has 1 more star? Mark under your answer. **2.** Count how many flowers. Write the number. **3.** How many counters? Write the number.

Name ________________________________

Problem Solving • Tell How Many Objects Without Counting

Essential Question How can you tell how many using the strategy *use a model*?

Learning Objective You will use the strategy *use a model* to tell how many objects there are without counting.

Unlock the Problem

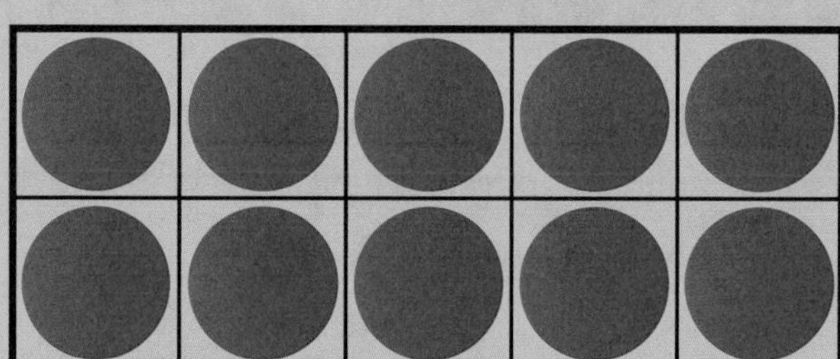

DIRECTIONS Look at each ten frame. Without counting, write how many counters there are in each one. Explain to a friend how you know.

Try Another Problem

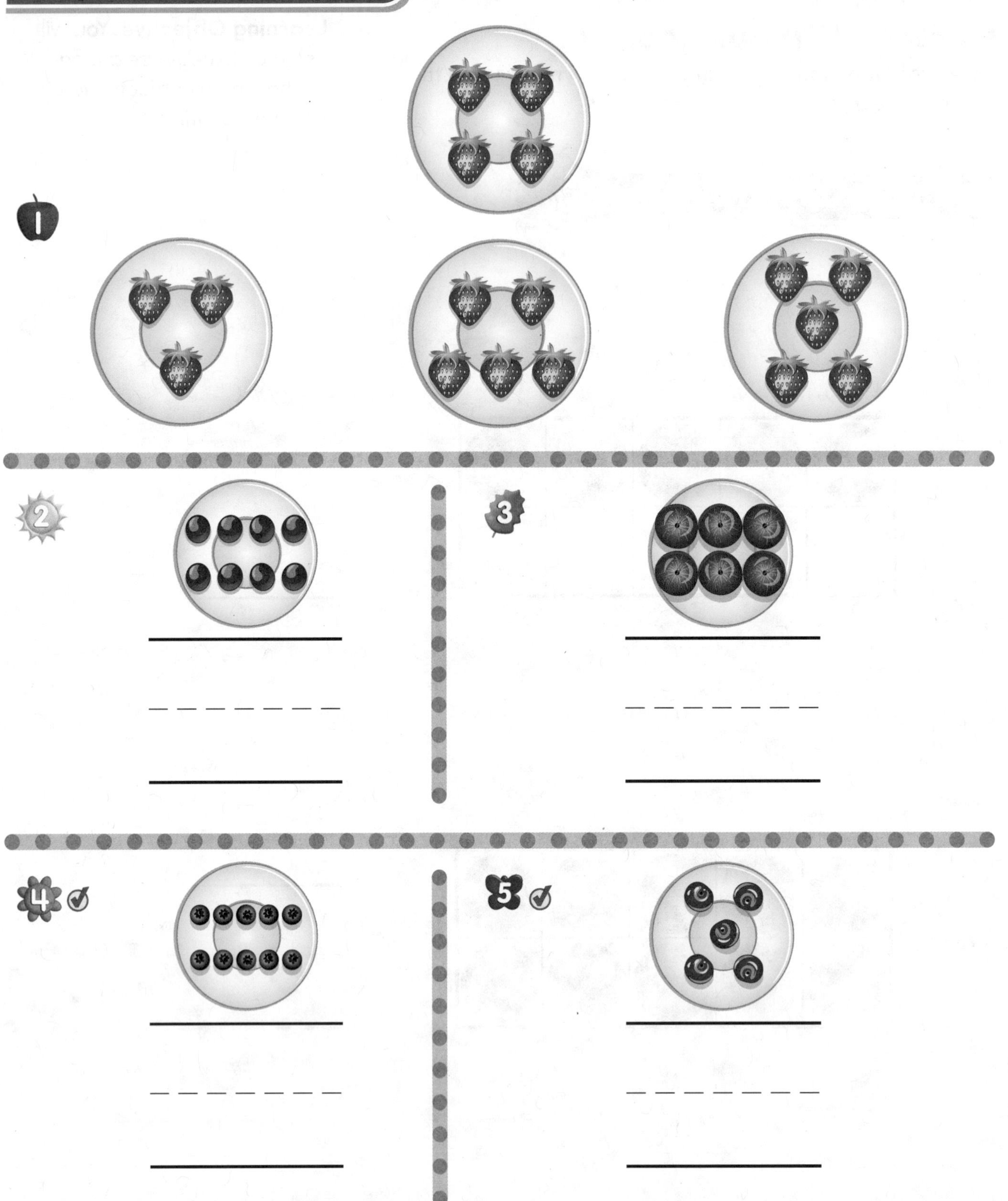

DIRECTIONS 1. Look at the plate at the top of the page. It has 4 berries. Without counting, mark an X on the plates that have more than 4 berries. **2–5.** Look at the fruit on each plate. Without counting, write how many.

Name ______________________

Share and Show

6

7

8

9

10

11

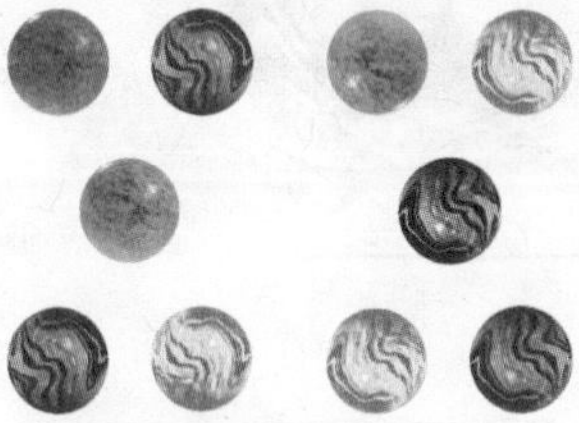

DIRECTIONS 6–11. Look at the marbles. Without counting, write how many.

On Your Own Real World

WRITE Math

12

13

14

15

16

DIRECTIONS 12–16. Sofia took a quick look at the eggs in some nests. Without counting, write how many eggs she saw in each nest. Tell a friend about the eggs in Exercise 16.

HOME CONNECTION • Place 10 or fewer objects, such as beans or coins, in different familiar arrangements. Use domino dot arrangements or rows of 5 or fewer. Then ask your child to tell how many without counting.

Name ______________________

Problem Solving • Tell How Many Objects Without Counting

Learning Objective You will use the strategy *use a model* to tell how many objects there are without counting.

1

2

3

4

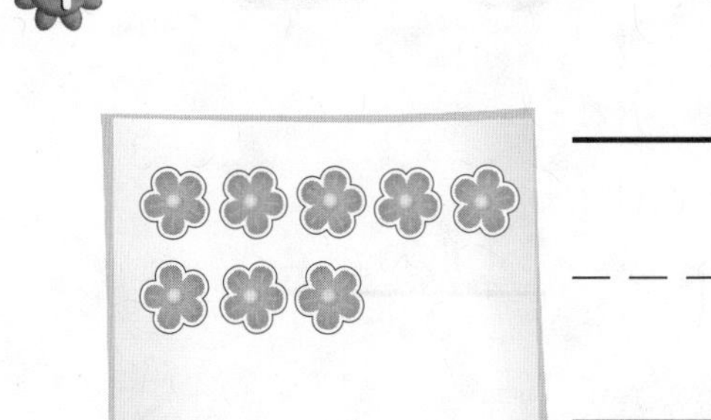

5

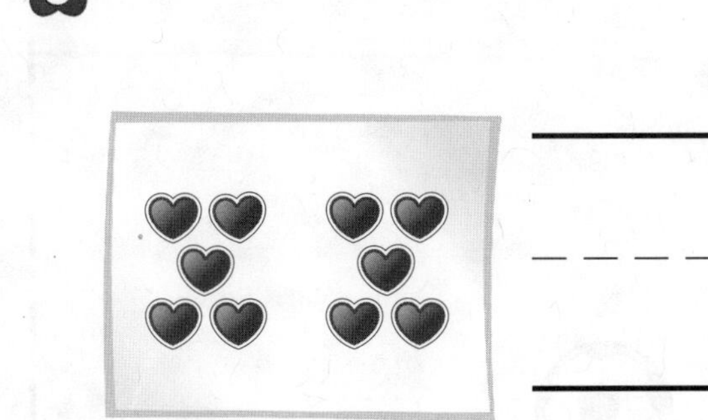

6

DIRECTIONS 1–6. Look at the stickers on each paper. Without counting, write how many.

Lesson Check

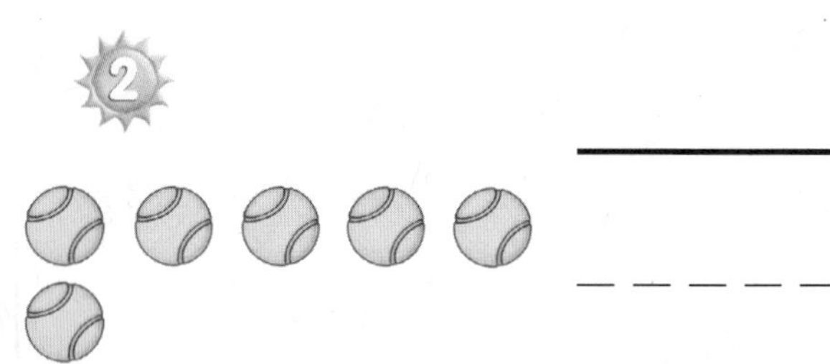

Spiral Review

       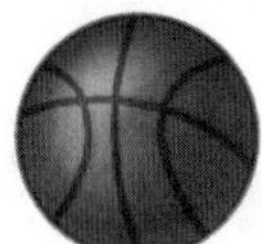

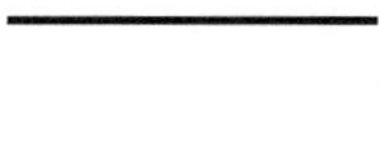

  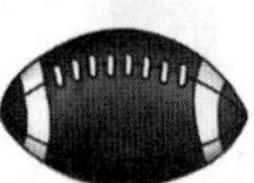 

DIRECTIONS 1–2. Look at the tennis balls. Without counting, write how many. **3.** Olivia puts eight basketballs into equal groups in two bins. How many basketballs does she put in each bin? Use cubes to model. Draw the groups. Write how many. **4.** Draw lines to match the footballs and soccer balls. Circle the group that has more.

Name ___________________________

One More and One Less

Essential Question How do you find the number that is one more or one less than a given number?

Learning Objective You will find one more and one less than a number.

Listen and Draw Real World

______ 10 ______

DIRECTIONS Place 10 counters in the ten frame. Take one counter away. Write the number that is one less than 10. Place 10 new counters in the ten frame. Add one more counter. Write the number that is one more than 10.

Share and Show

1

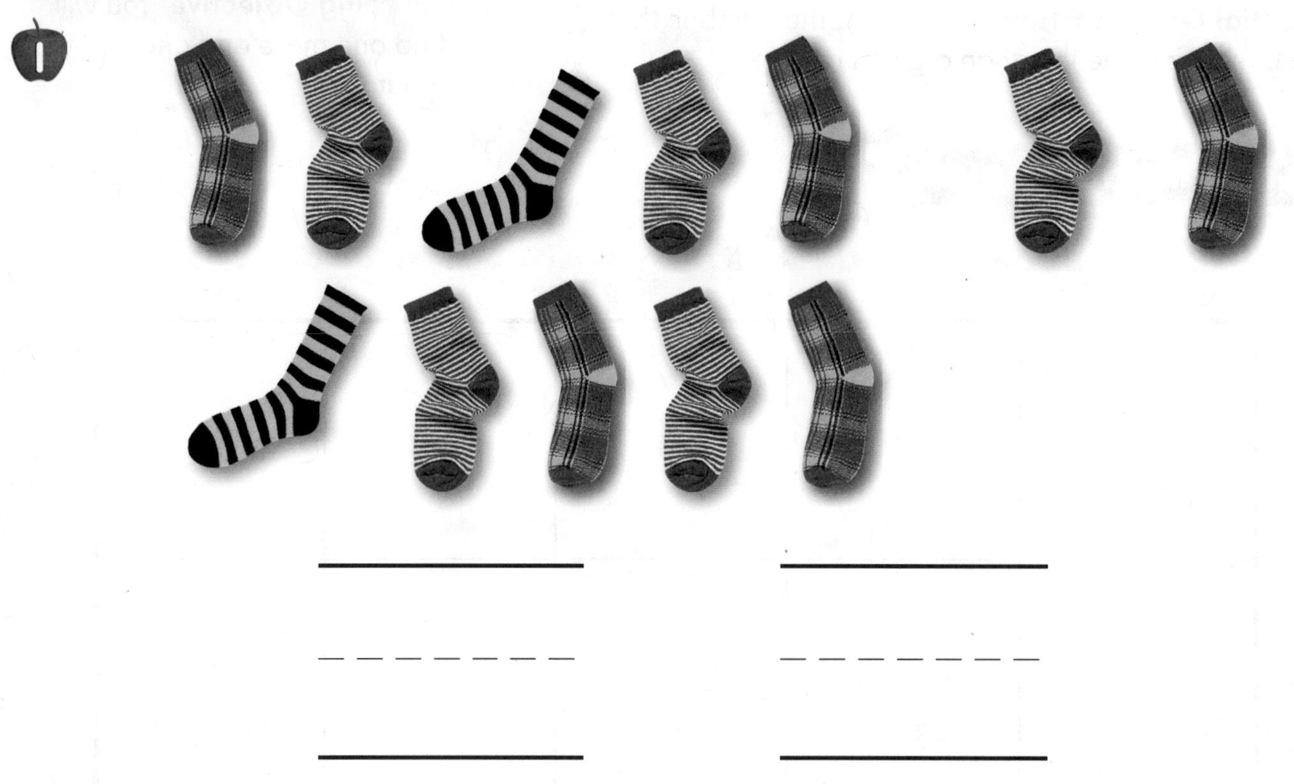

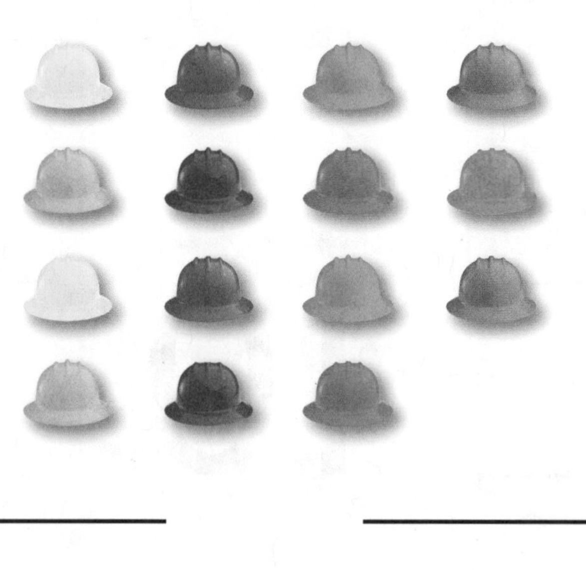

DIRECTIONS 1. There are 12 socks. Write the number that is one more than 12. Write the number that is one less than 12. 2. There are 15 hats. Write the number that is one more than 15. Write the number that is one less than 15.

Name ______________________

3

17

4

14

5

19

DIRECTIONS 3–5. Look at the number. Write the number that is one less. Write the number that is one more.

Problem Solving • Applications Real World

6

WRITE Math

7

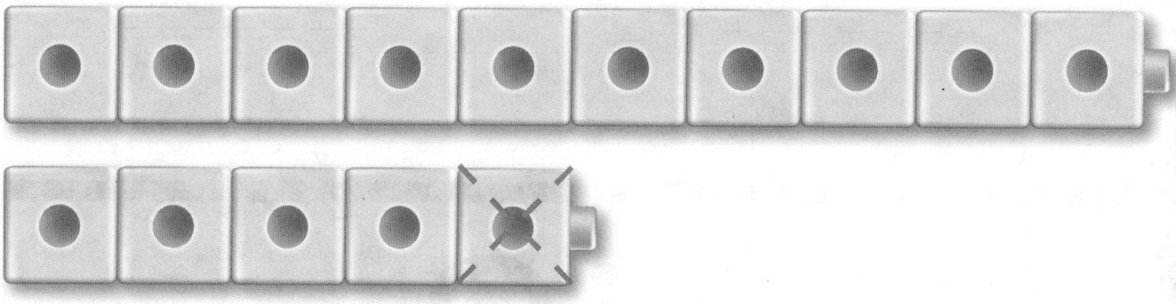

10 ○

14 ○

DIRECTIONS 6. Adele has 10 hats. Seamus has one more hat than Adele. Draw to show how many hats Seamus has. 7. Choose the correct answer. There are 15 cubes. What number is one less?

HOME ACTIVITY • Show your child a set of 11 to 20 objects such as spoons or forks. Have your child create a set of objects that shows one more or one less.

Name ______________________

One More and One Less

Learning Objective You will find one more and one less than a number.

1

19

2

16

3

18

DIRECTIONS 1–3. Look at the number. Write the number that is one less. Write the number that is one more.

Lesson Check

1

○ 15 ○ 17

○ 10 ○ 12

Spiral Review

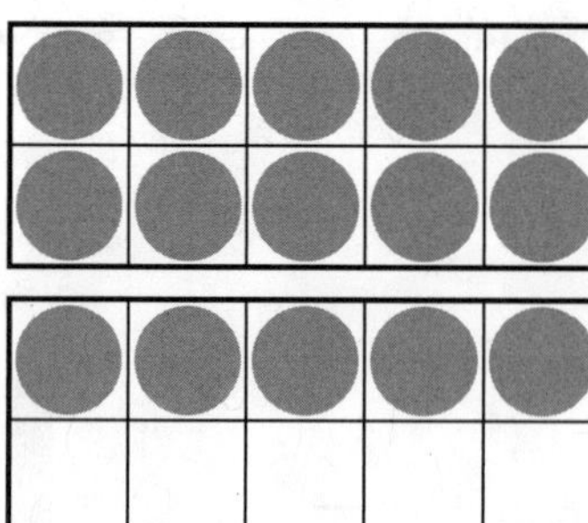

DIRECTIONS Choose the correct answer. **1.** There are 16 cubes. What number is one less? **2.** There are 11 stars. What number is one more? **3.** Count how many books. Write the number. **4.** How many counters? Write the number.

Name ___________________________

Compare Two Numbers to 20

Essential Question How can you compare two numbers between 1 and 20?

Learning Objective You will compare the values of two numbers between 1 and 20 presented as written numerals.

Listen and Draw

Real World

17

17 is less than 18

17 is greater than 18

18

18 is less than 17

18 is greater than 17

DIRECTIONS Look at the numbers. As you count forward does 17 come before or after 18? Is it greater or less than 18? Circle the words that describe the numbers when comparing them.

Share and Show

1

13 18

2

20 5

3

6 14

4

17 19

5

10 20

DIRECTIONS 1. Look at the numbers. Think about the counting order as you compare the numbers. Trace the circle around the greater number. **2–5.** Look at the numbers. Think about the counting order as you compare the numbers. Circle the greater number.

Name ____________________

6

12 4

7

15 13

8

18 9

9

10 17

10

6 18

DIRECTIONS 6–10. Look at the numbers. Think about the counting order as you compare the numbers. Circle the number that is less.

Problem Solving • Applications

Real World

WRITE Math

11

12

DIRECTIONS 11. John has a number of apples that is greater than 15 and less than 17. Cody has a number of apples that is two less than 18. Write how many apples each boy has. Compare the numbers. Tell a friend about the numbers. 12. Write two numbers between 11 and 20. Tell a friend about the two numbers.

HOME ACTIVITY • Write the numbers 10 to 20 on individual pieces of paper. Select two numbers and ask your child to compare the numbers and tell which number is greater and which number is less.

Name ______________________________

Compare Two Numbers to 20

Learning Objective You will compare the values of two numbers between 1 and 20 presented as written numerals.

1. 8 15

2. 10 17

3. 16 19

4. 16 14

5. 8 17

6. 5 13

DIRECTIONS 1–3. Look at the numbers. Think about the counting order as you compare the numbers. Circle the greater number. 4–6. Look at the numbers. Think about the counting order as you compare the numbers. Circle the number that is less.

Lesson Check

17 11

Spiral Review

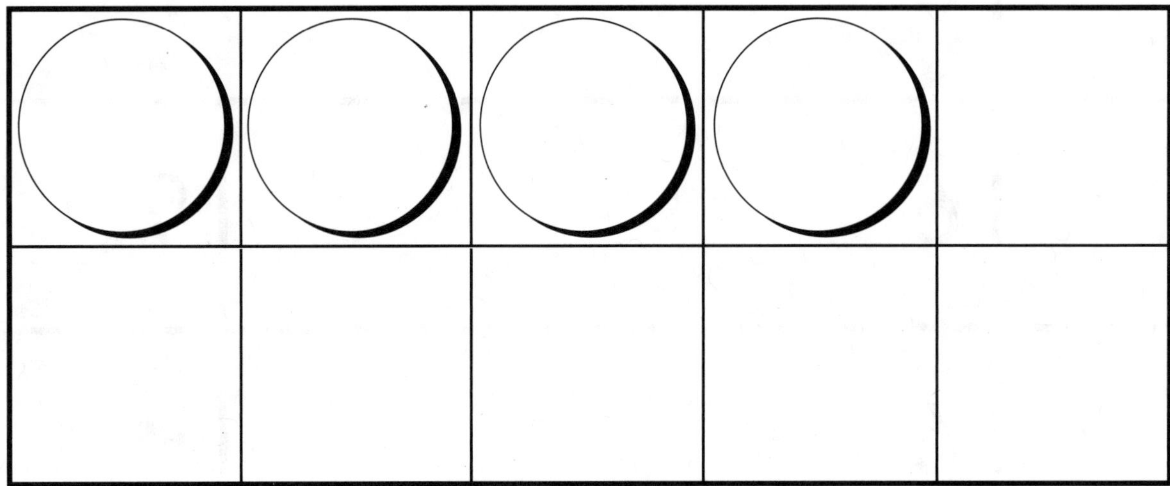

DIRECTIONS 1. Look at the numbers. Think about the counting order as you compare the numbers. Circle the greater number. **2.** How many more counters would you place in the ten frame to show a way to make 8? Draw the counters. **3.** How many birds are there? Write the number.

Name ____________________

Above, Below, Over, and Under

Essential Question How can you describe objects using the positional words *above*, *below*, *over*, and *under*?

Learning Objective You will use the position words *above*, *below*, *over*, and *under* to describe objects.

Listen and Draw Real World

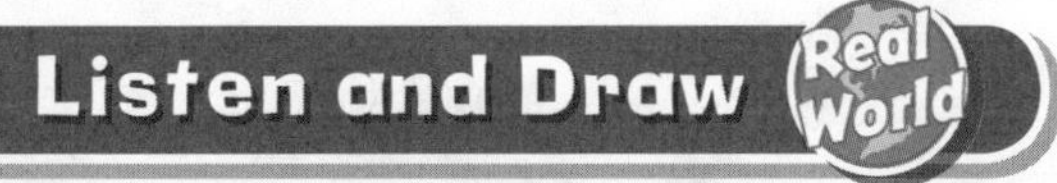

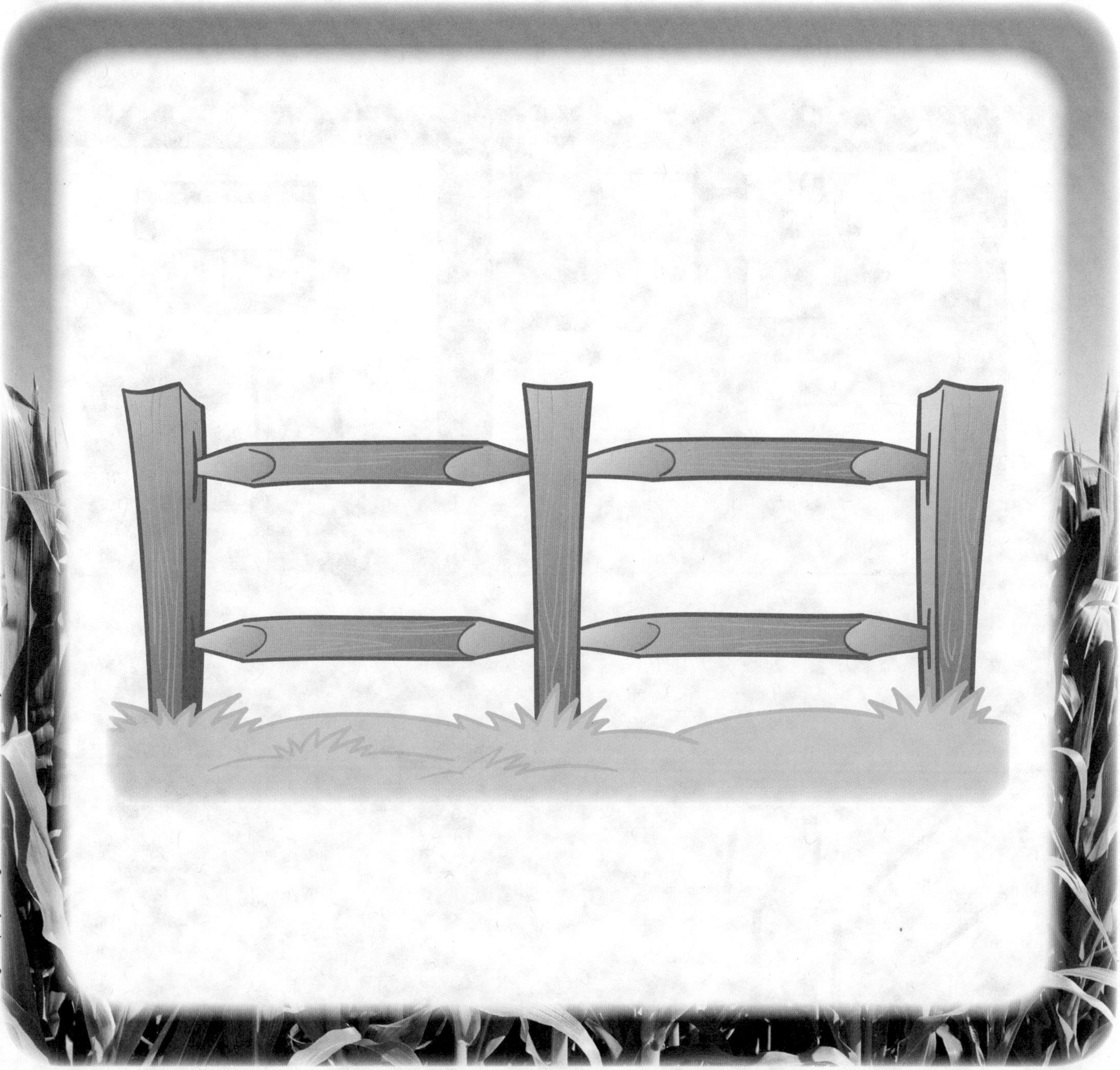

DIRECTIONS Place a red cube above the fence and a blue cube below the fence. Draw and color the cubes. Mark an X over the fence and draw a circle under the fence.

Share and Show

1

DIRECTIONS 1. Place a red cube below the water. Place a red cube under the ladder. Use red to draw these cubes. Place a blue cube over the window. Place a blue cube above the horses. Use blue to draw these cubes.

Name ______________________________

DIRECTIONS 2. Place a red cube above the pond. Place a blue cube below the table. Draw and color the cubes. 3. Place a blue cube under the tree. Place a red cube over the house. Draw and color the cubes.

Problem Solving • Applications Real World

WRITE Math

4

DIRECTIONS 4. Look at the birds. Which bird is over the corn plants? Mark an X on that bird. Look for the corn. Circle the corn that is below the ground. Which fox is above the ground? Mark an X on that fox.

HOME ACTIVITY • Tell your child you are thinking of something in the room that is over or under another object. Have your child tell you what the object is.

Name ______________________________

Above, Below, Over, and Under

Learning Objective You will use the position words *above*, *below*, *over*, and *under* to describe objects.

1

2

DIRECTIONS 1. Place a red cube above the trees. Place a blue cube below the table. Draw and color the cubes. 2. Place a red cube under the ball. Place a blue cube over the swing set. Draw and color the cubes.

Lesson Check

1

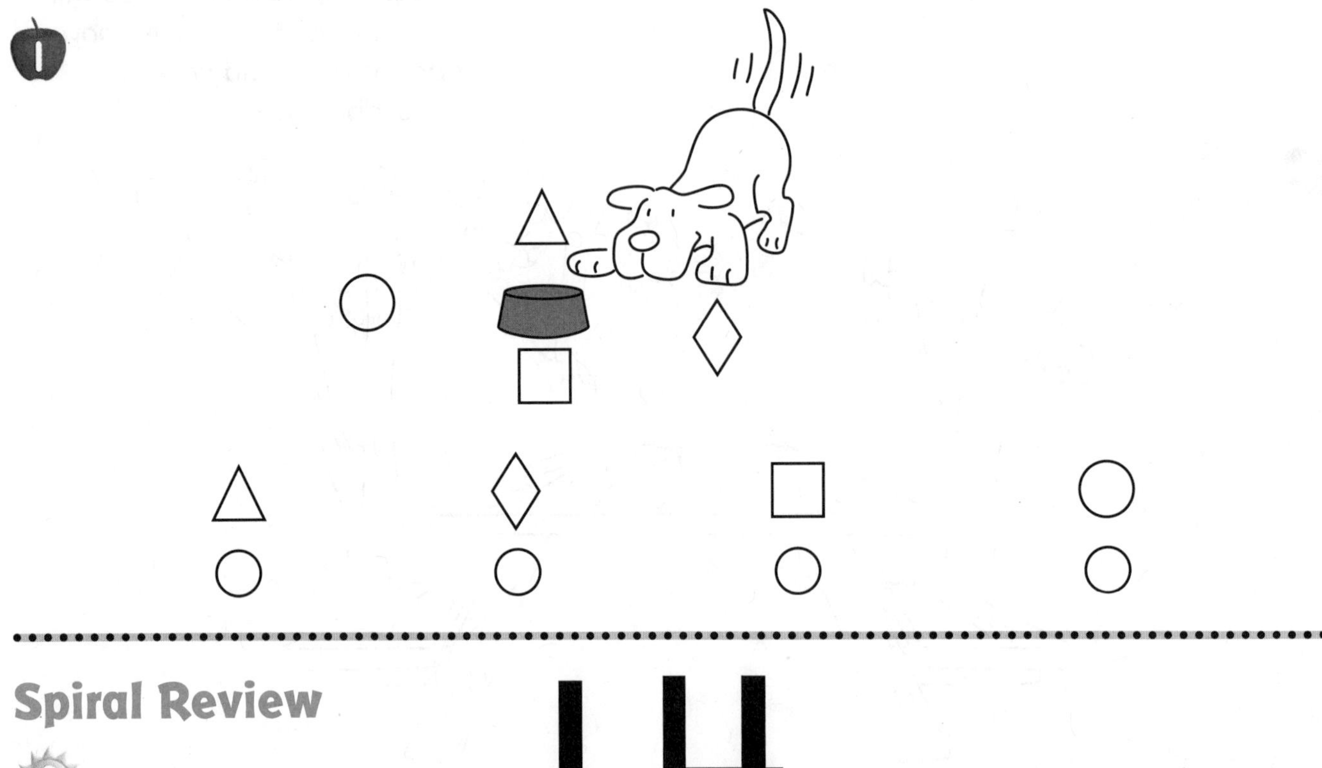

Spiral Review

2

14
fourteen

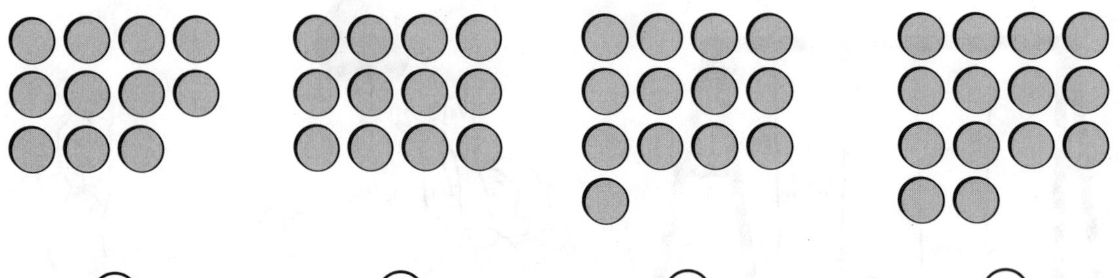

3

DIRECTIONS 1. Which shape is above the water bowl? Mark under your answer. 2. Which set has 14? Mark under your answer. 3. How many skateboards? Write the number.

Name ______________________________

Beside, Next To, and Between

Essential Question How can you describe objects using the positional words *beside*, *next to*, and *between*?

Learning Objective You will use the position words *beside*, *next to*, and *between* to describe objects.

Listen and Draw Real World

DIRECTIONS Which color cube is between the blue cubes? Which color cube is next to the green cube? Which color cube is beside the yellow cube? On the other shelf, place a red cube beside a blue cube. Now place a yellow cube between the red cube and the blue cube. Draw and color the cubes.

Share and Show

1

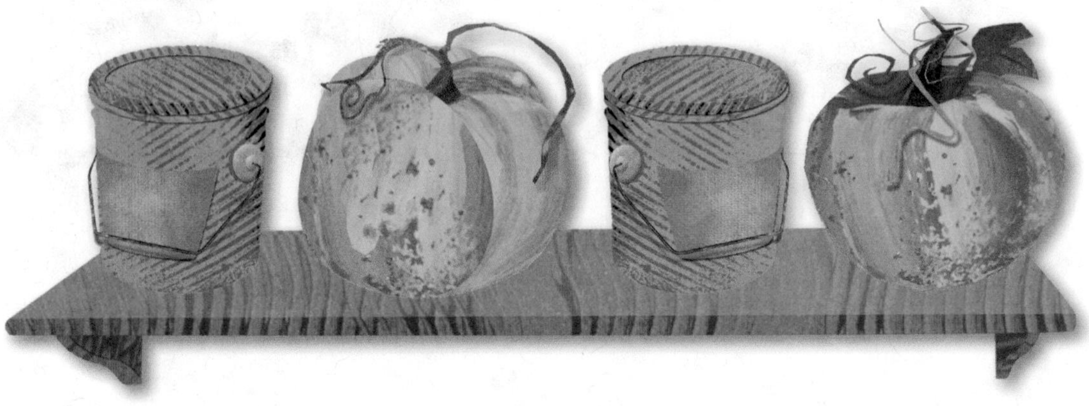

DIRECTIONS **1.** Place a cube on the football that is next to the basket. Mark an X on that football. **2.** Place a cube on the pumpkin that is between two paint cans. Mark an X on that pumpkin. **3.** Place a cube on the ball that is beside a cap. Mark an X on that ball.

Name ____________________

4

DIRECTIONS 4. Place a cube on the pumpkin that is between two other pumpkins. Mark an X on that pumpkin. Place a cube on the pumpkin next to the hay. Circle that pumpkin. Place a cube next to the tree. Draw the cube.

Problem Solving • Applications Real World

WRITE Math

5

6

DIRECTIONS 5. Circle the watering can that is between the pumpkins. Mark an X on the pumpkin that is next to the hay. 6. Draw to show objects that are beside, next to, and between other objects. Tell about your drawing.

HOME ACTIVITY • Use language such as *beside*, *next to*, and *between* to describe the position of one object in relation to another.

Name ____________________

Beside, Next To, and Between

Learning Objective You will use the position words *beside*, *next to*, and *between* to describe objects.

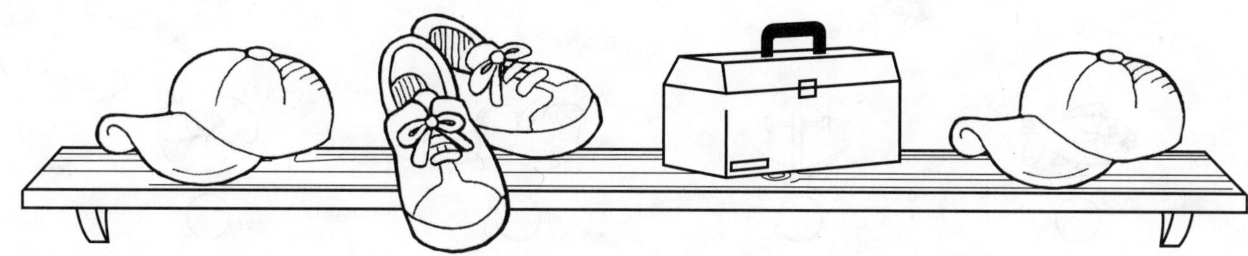

3

DIRECTIONS 1. Place a cube on the the cap that is beside the toolbox. Circle that cap. Place a cube on the cap that is next to the shoes. Mark an X on that cap. **2.** Place a cube on the football that is between two hats. Mark an X on that football. Place a cube on the football that is beside the skates. Circle that football. **3.** Place a cube on the watering can that is next to the shoes. Mark an X on that watering can.

Lesson Check

  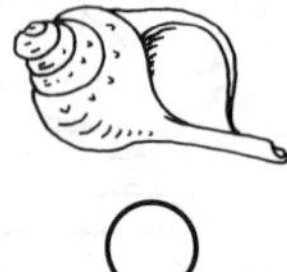 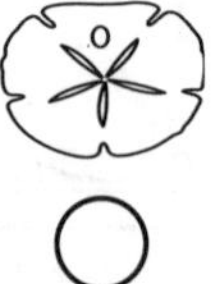

○ ○ ○ ○

Spiral Review

○ ○ ○ ○ ○ ○ ○ ○ ○ ○

○ ○ ○ ○ ○ ○ ○ ○ ○ ○

17 18 19 20

○ ○ ○ ○

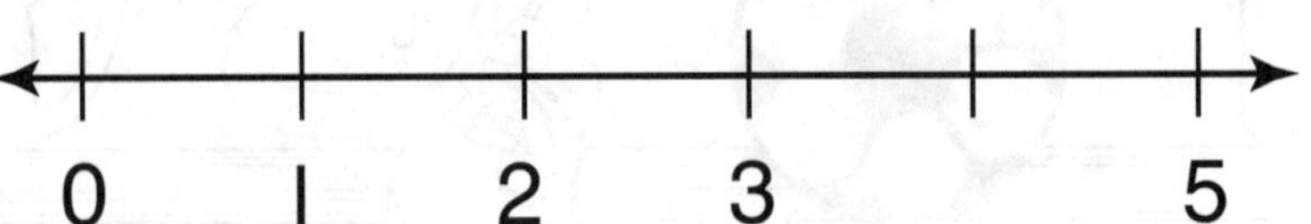

3 4 5 6

○ ○ ○ ○

DIRECTIONS 1. Which object is between the two fish? Mark under your answer. 2. How many cubes? Mark under your answer. 3. What number comes before 5? Mark under your answer.

Name ______________________________

Inside and Outside

Essential Question How can you describe objects using the positional words *inside* and *outside*?

Learning Objective You will use the position words *inside* and *outside* to describe objects.

Listen and Draw Real World

DIRECTIONS Place a red counter inside the fence. Place a yellow counter outside the fence. Draw and color the counters.

Share and Show

1

2

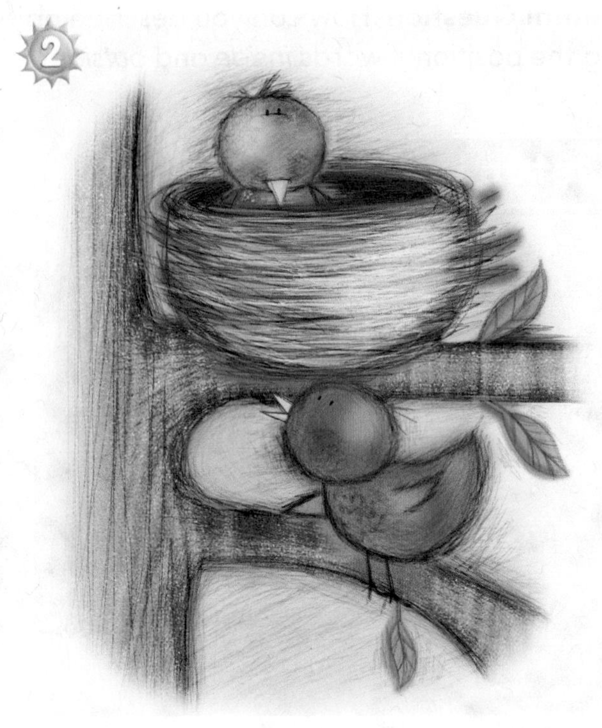

3

4

DIRECTIONS 1. Place a counter on the child who is outside the house. Circle that child. **2.** Place a counter on the bird that is inside the nest. Circle that bird. **3.** Place a counter on the squirrel that is inside the tree. Circle that squirrel. **4.** Place a counter on the dog that is outside the dog house. Circle that dog.

Name ___________________________

5

DIRECTIONS 5. Place a red counter inside the basket. Use red to draw the counter. Place a yellow counter outside the basket. Use yellow to draw the counter.

Problem Solving • Applications Real World

WRITE Math

6

7

DIRECTIONS 6. Mark an X on the bucket that is inside the sandbox. Circle the shovel that is outside the sandbox. 7. Draw to show what you know about objects that are inside and outside other objects. Tell about your drawing.

HOME ACTIVITY • Give your child a block and a dish that is large enough to hold the block. Ask your child to place the block inside the dish. Then ask your child to place the block outside the dish.

Name ______________________________

Inside and Outside

Learning Objective You will use the position words *inside* and *outside* to describe objects.

1

DIRECTIONS 1. Place a counter on the white sheep inside the fence. Circle that sheep. Place a counter on the black sheep outside the fence. Mark an X on that sheep.

Lesson Check

1

Spiral Review

2

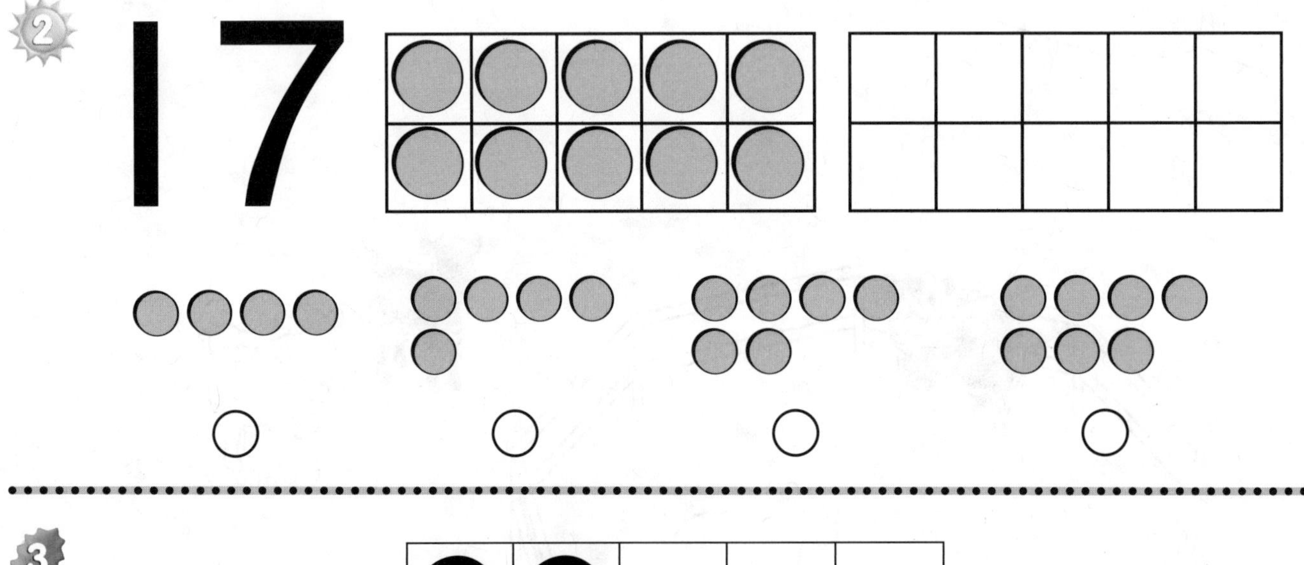

3

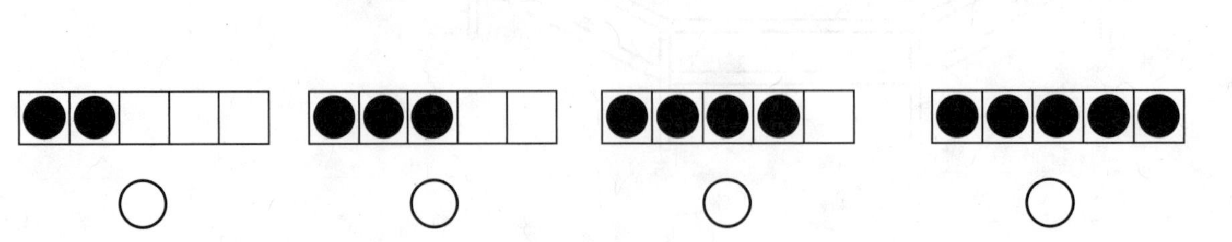

DIRECTIONS 1. What fruit is inside the basket? Mark under your answer. 2. How many more counters are needed to show 17? Mark under your answer. 3. Count and tell how many counters are in the five frame. Which set of counters has one more counter? Mark under your answer.

Name ______________________________

Position Words

Essential Question How can you use the terms *to the right of* and *to the left of* to describe positions of objects and shapes in space?

Learning Objective You will use the terms *to the right of* and *to the left of* to describe the positions of objects and shapes in space.

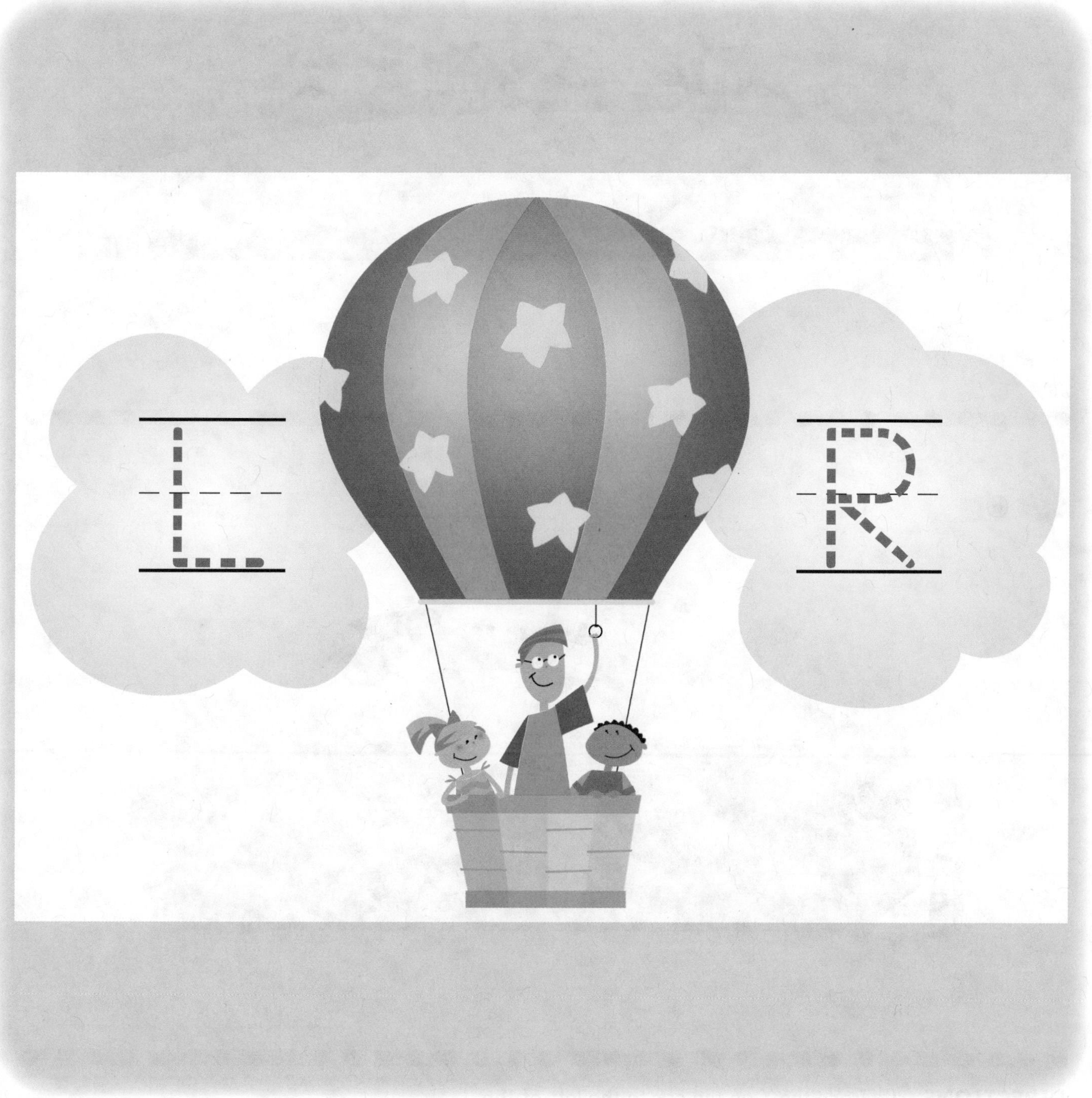

L

R

DIRECTIONS Trace the L on the cloud to the left of the hot air balloon. Trace the R on the cloud to the right of the hot air balloon.

Share and Show

DIRECTIONS 1. Trace the X on the car to the left of the blue car. Trace the circle on the car to the right of the blue car. 2. Mark an X on the fish to the left of the octopus. Circle the fish to the right of the octopus.

Name ______________________________

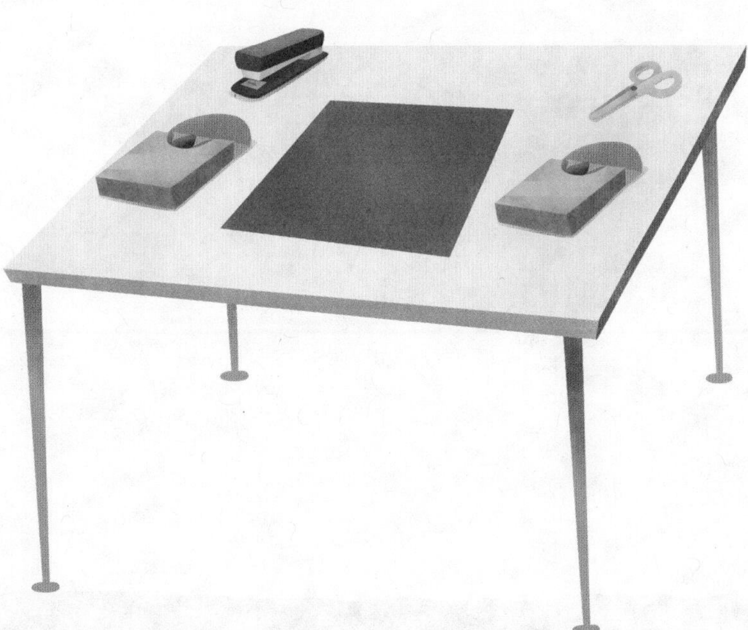

DIRECTIONS **3.** Mark an X on the girl to the right of the boy jumping. Circle the girl to the left of the boy jumping. **4.** Circle the crayons to the right of the paper. Mark an X on the crayons to the left of the paper.

Problem Solving • Applications Real World

5

WRITE Math

DIRECTIONS 5. Lily drew a tree between two houses. She colored the house on the right yellow and the house on the left orange. She drew a bird over the house. Draw what her picture might have looked like.

HOME CONNECTION • Ask your child to name an object in the room that is on his or her right, then an object that is to his or her left. Then ask him or her to tell you about different objects in the room using the terms *to the right of* and *to the left of*.

Name ____________________________________

Position Words

Learning Objective You will use the terms *to the right of* and *to the left of* to describe the positions of objects and shapes in space.

1

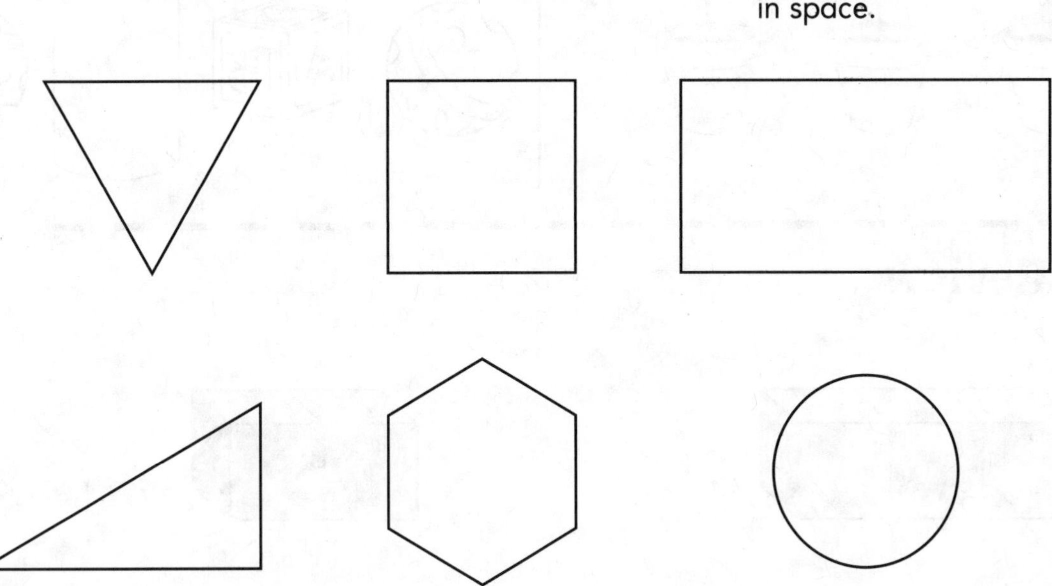

DIRECTIONS 1. Mark an X on the shape to the right of the square. Circle the shape to the left of the square. **2.** Use green to color the tree on the left of the school. Use brown to color the tree on the right of the school.

Lesson Check

1

2

Spiral Review

3

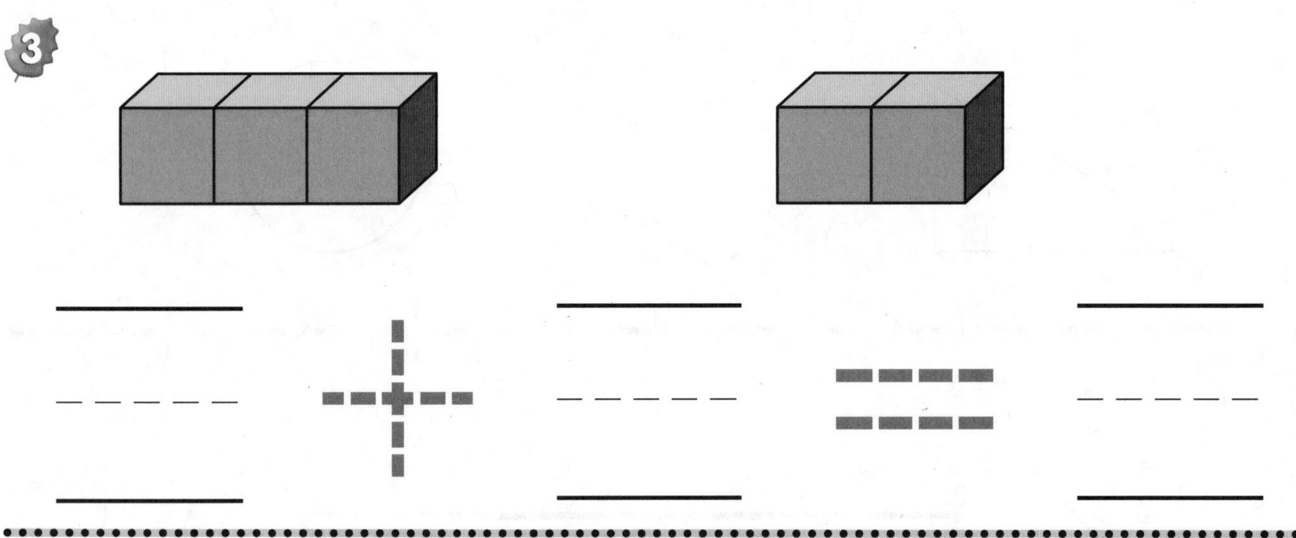

4

DIRECTIONS 1. Point to the flower pot between two other flower pots. Use red to color the flower on the left. Use yellow to color the flower on the right. 2. Use green to color the ball to the left of the cube. Use orange to color the ball to the right of the cylinder. 3. Noah has three blocks. He gets two more. How many blocks does he have now? Complete the addition sentence. 4. What fruit is inside the basket? Mark under your answer.

Name ________________________________

More Position Words

Essential Question How can you use the terms *up*, *down*, *near*, and *far* to describe positions of objects and shapes in space?

Learning Objective You will use the terms *up*, *down*, *near*, and *far* to describe the positions of objects and shapes in space.

Listen and Draw Real World

DIRECTIONS Trace the circle on the child that is going up the slide. Trace the X on the child that is going down the slide. Trace the X on the tree that is far from the swings. Trace the circle around the tree that is near the swings.

Share and Show

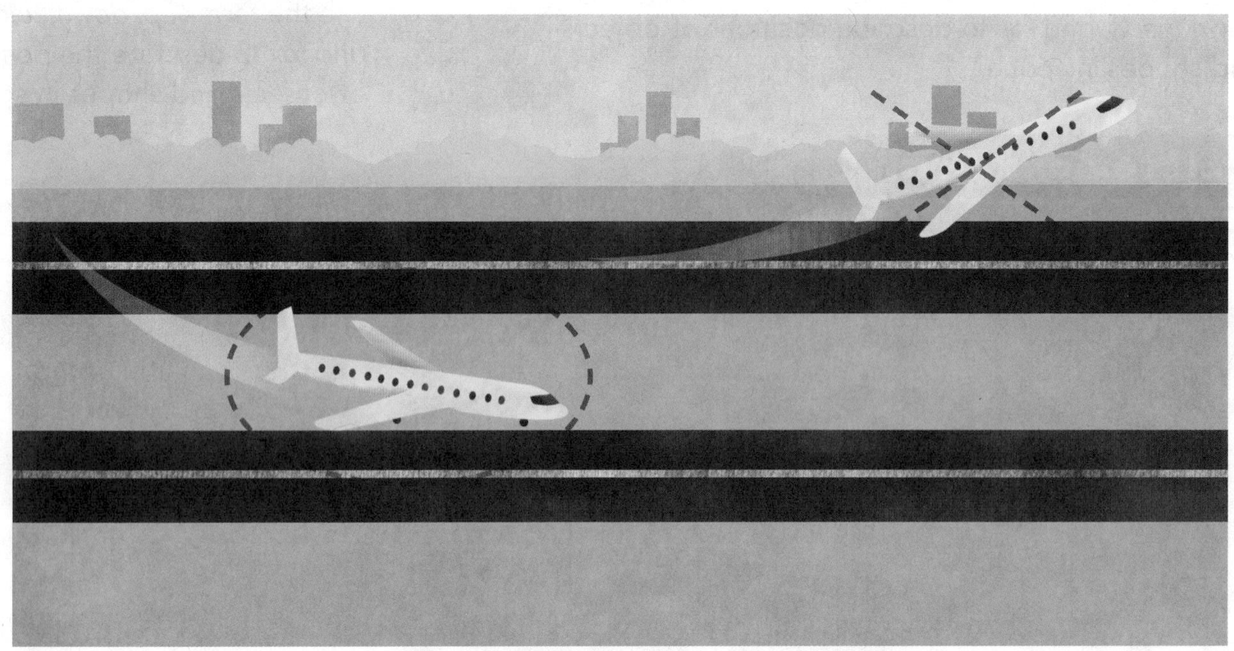

DIRECTIONS 1. Trace the X on the plane going up in the air. Trace the circle on the plane that is going down. **2.** Mark an X on the bird that is far from the house. Circle the bird that is near the house.

Name ______________________________

DIRECTIONS 3. Mark an X on the child going down the slide. Circle the child going up the slide. 4. Mark an X on the marble that is far from the red marble. Draw a circle around the marble that is near the blue marble. Draw to show an object near and an object far from the marbles. Use the terms *near* and *far* to tell a friend about your drawing.

Problem Solving • Applications Real World

5

WRITE Math

DIRECTIONS 5. Draw to complete the picture. Use red to color the shirt of the boy that is up. Use blue to color the shirt of the boy that is down. Next, draw a bird flying far from the boys. Last, draw a football near the boys. Use the words *up*, *down*, *near*, and *far* to tell a friend about your picture.

HOME CONNECTION • Ask your child to name two objects in the room that are far from him or her. Then, have your child name two objects that are near him or her. Next, have your child demonstrate something going up, and then something going down.

Name ______________________________

More Position Words

Learning Objective You will use the terms *up, down, near, and far* to describe the positions of objects and shapes in space.

DIRECTIONS 1. Mark an X on the person going down the escalator. Circle the person going up the escalator. 2. Mark an X on an object that is far from the children. Circle an object that is near the boy. Use the terms *near* and *far* to tell someone about some of the other objects.

Lesson Check

Spiral Review

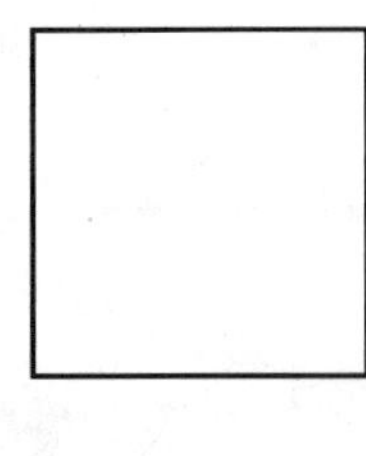

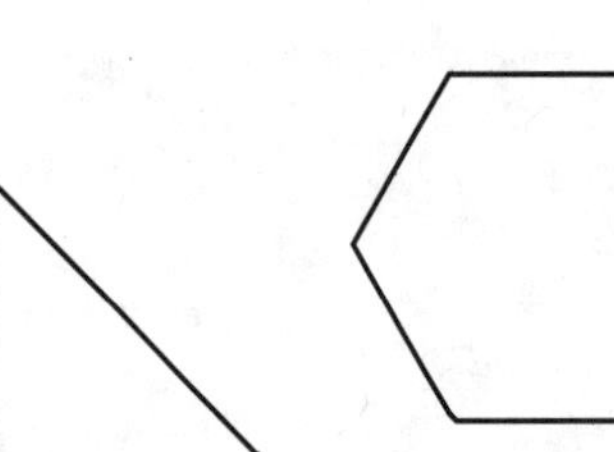

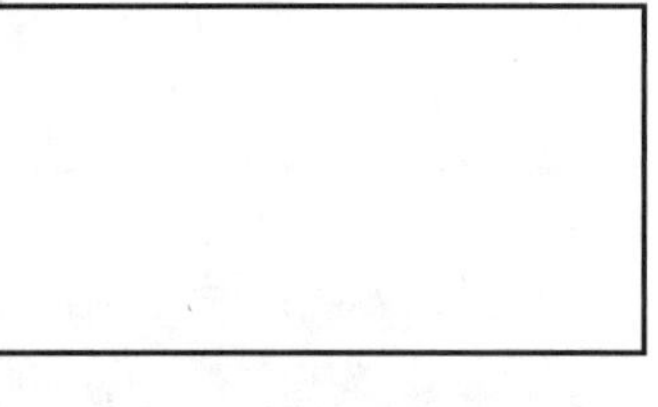

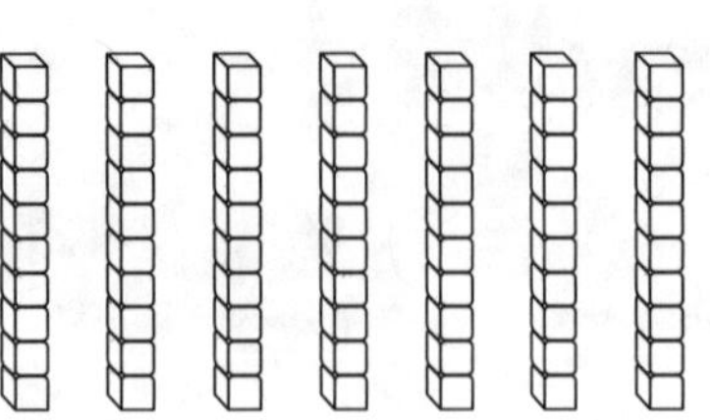

7 10 70

DIRECTIONS 1. Mark an X on the car going down the roller coaster. Circle the car going up the roller coaster. 2. Mark an X on the tree near the park bench. Circle the tree that is far from the park bench. 3. Circle the triangle. 4. Count by tens. Circle how many.

Name ______________________________

Explore Capacity

Essential Question How can you explore to find capacity?

Learning Objective You will explore to find capacity.

about 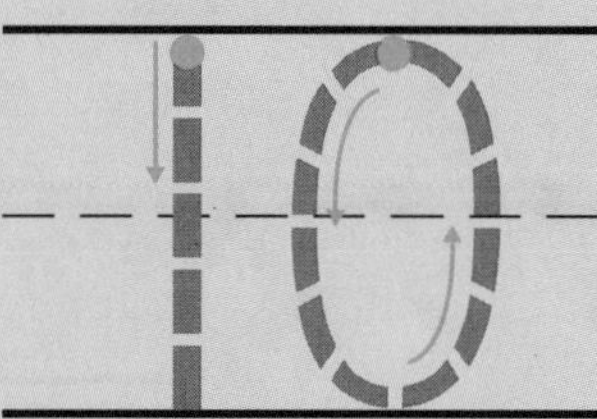 handfuls

DIRECTIONS Kayla wants to know how many handfuls of sand will fill the cup. She counts as she pours each one in. She draws dots to help her keep count. Trace the number of handfuls.

Share and Show

about 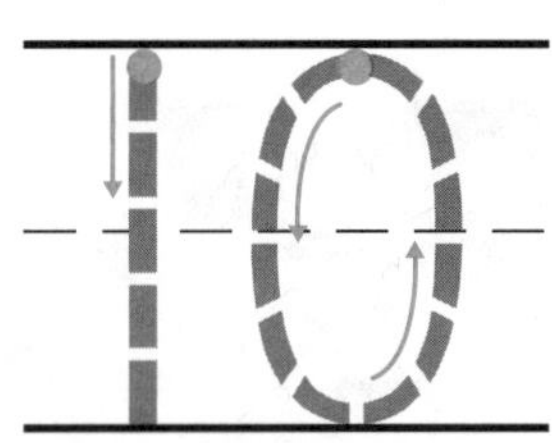 handfuls

about 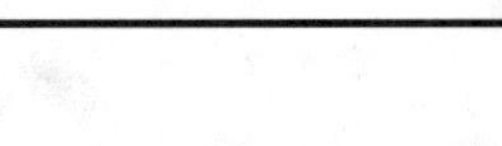 ______ handfuls

about  ______ handfuls

about  ______ handfuls

DIRECTIONS Use cups like the ones shown. Fill each cup with handfuls of rice or beans **1.** Trace the number that show about how many handfuls. **2–4.** Write about how many handfuls each cup holds.

Name ______________________

5

about ______

6

about ______

7

about ______

8

about ______

DIRECTIONS 5–8. Use containers like the ones shown. Fill each container with cups of rice or beans. Write about how many cups each container holds.

Problem Solving • Applications 

9

WRITE Math

Madison

about ______ handfuls

Jacob

about ______

DIRECTIONS 9. Madison and Jacob want to find the capacity of the blue cup. Madison uses handfuls of rice. Jacob uses spoonfuls of rice. Will they get the same answer? Use handfuls and spoonfuls of rice and a cup to find out. Explain why the answers are the same or different.

HOME CONNECTION • Provide two different-sized small containers and a bag of rice or beans. Ask your child to use handfuls of rice or beans to find the capacity of each container.

Name ____________________

Explore Capacity

Learning Objective You will explore to find capacity.

1

about

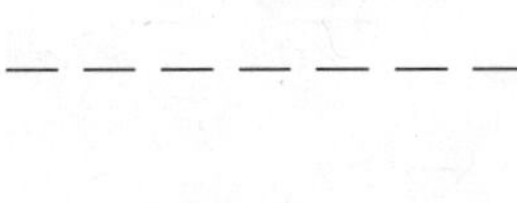

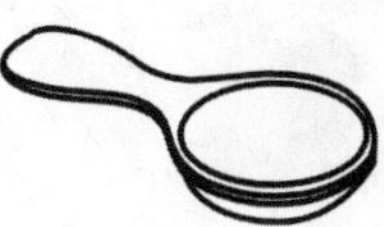

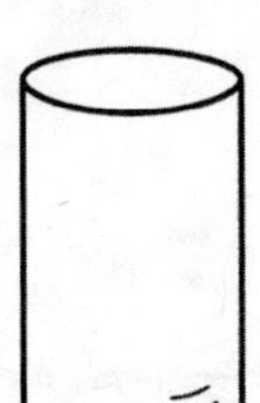

about

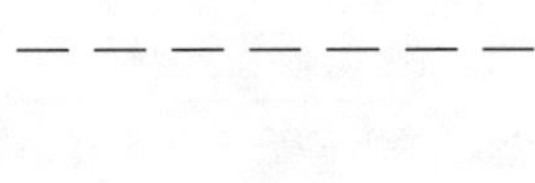

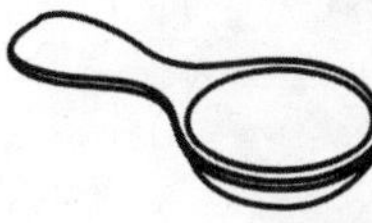

about

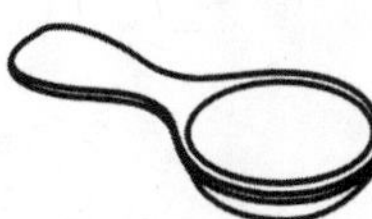

about

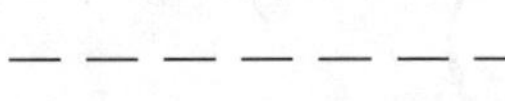

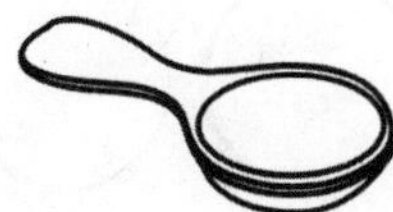

DIRECTIONS 1–4. Use containers like the ones shown. Fill each container with spoonfuls of rice or beans. Write about how many spoonfuls each container holds.

Lesson Check

about

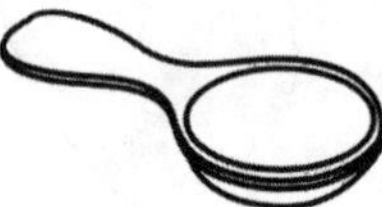

about

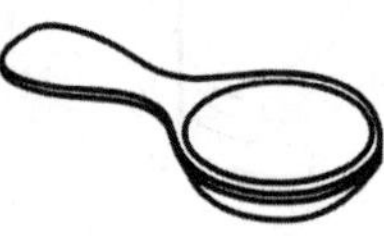

Spiral Review

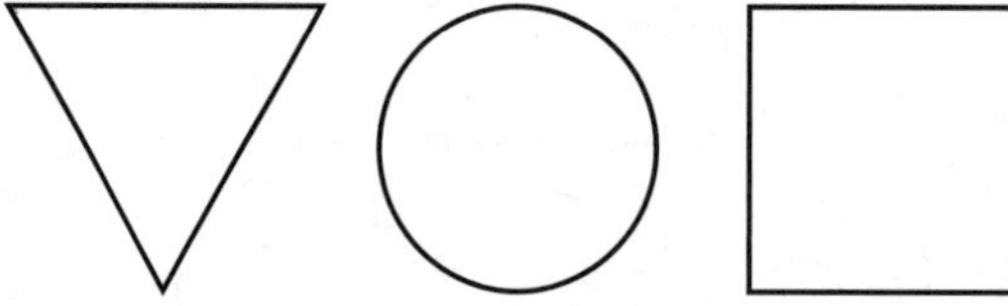

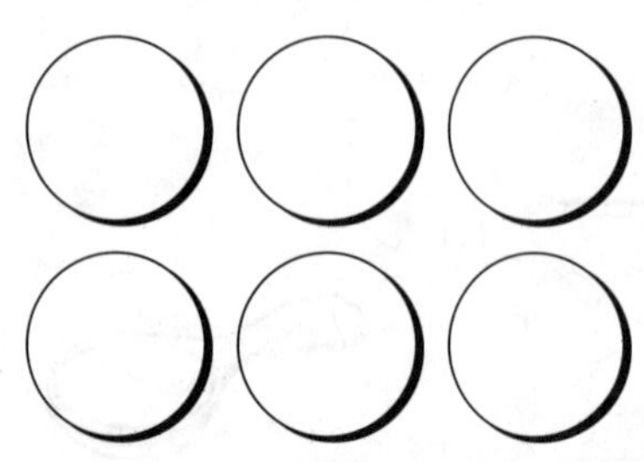

DIRECTIONS 1–2. Use containers like the ones shown. Fill each container with spoonfuls of rice or beans. Write about how many spoonfuls each container holds. **3.** Circle the shape to the right of the circle. Mark an X on the shape to the left of the circle. **4.** Look at the counters. Without counting, write how many.

Name ______________________________

Compare Capacity

Essential Question How can you compare the capacity of two containers to see which holds more?

Learning Objective You will compare the capacity of two containers to see which holds more.

Listen and Draw Real World

DIRECTIONS Olivia has a dropper and a cup. She wants to find other containers that hold about the same amount as these objects. Trace the containers she might find.

Share and Show

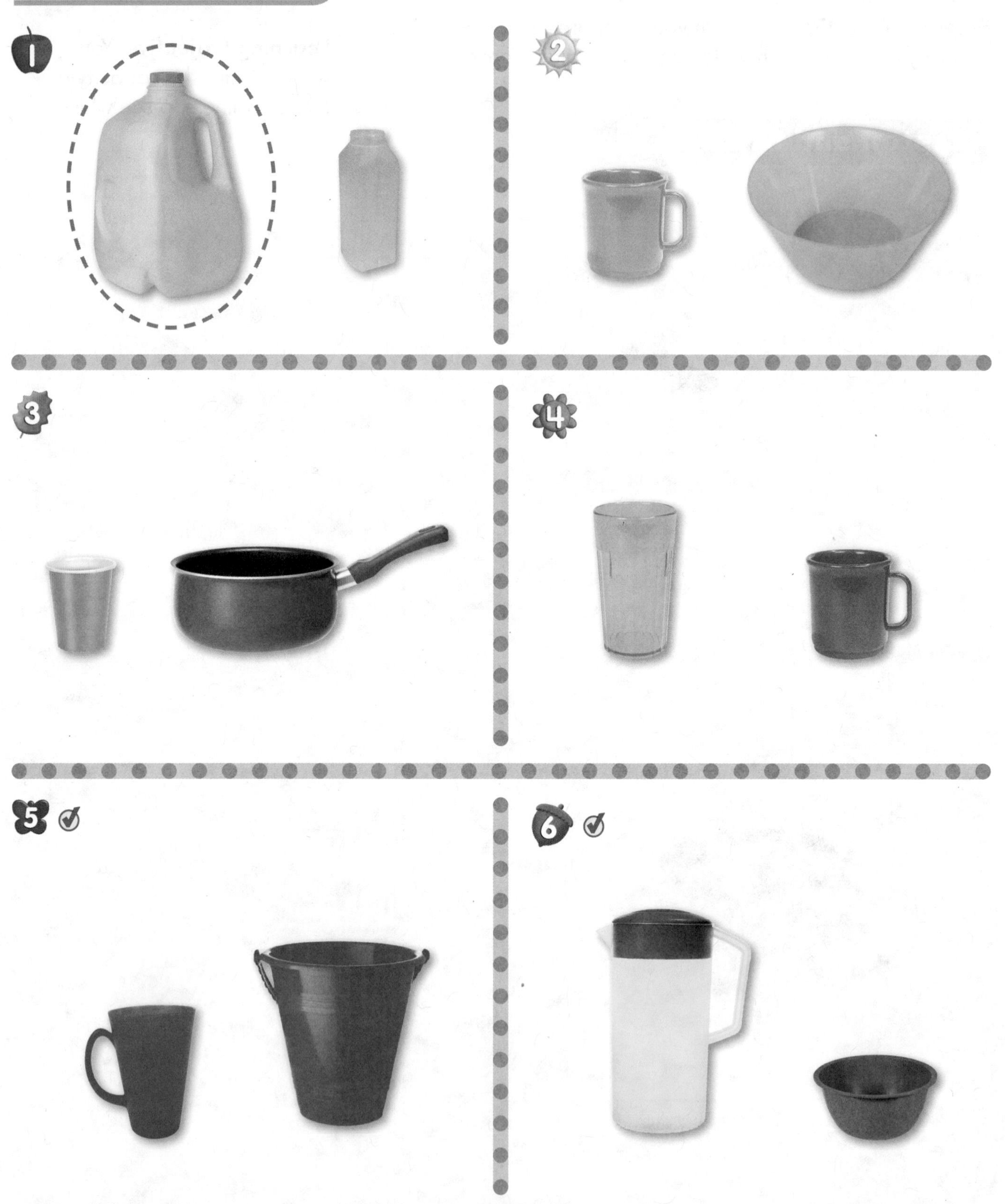

DIRECTIONS Fill one container with beans or rice. Pour it into the other container. **1.** Trace the circle to show the container that holds more. **2–4.** Circle the container that holds more. **5–6.** Mark an X on the container that holds less.

Name ________________________________

7

8

9

10

11

12

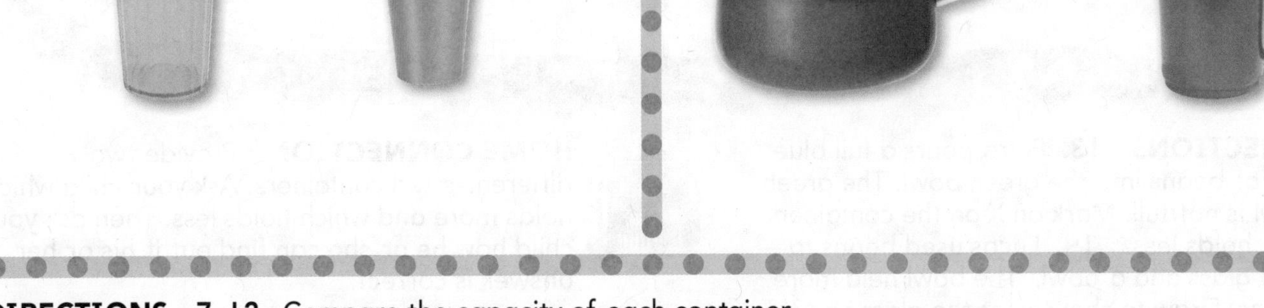

DIRECTIONS 7–12. Compare the capacity of each container. Circle the container that holds more. Mark an X on the container that holds less.

Problem Solving • Applications Real World

WRITE Math

13

14

DIRECTIONS 13. Petra pours a full blue cup of beans into the green bowl. The green bowl is not full. Mark an X on the container that holds less. 14. Lucas used beans to fill a glass and a bowl. The bowl held more beans. Draw to show what the glass and the bowl might look like.

HOME CONNECTION • Provide two different-sized containers. Ask your child which holds more and which holds less. Then ask your child how he or she can find out if his or her answer is correct.

Name ________________________________

Compare Capacity

Learning Objective You will compare the capacity of two containers to see which holds more.

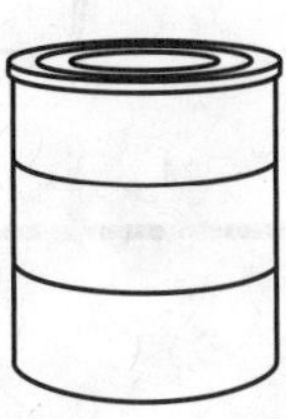

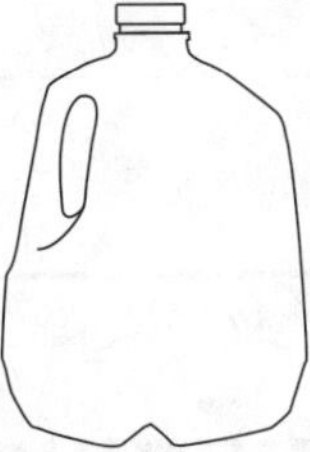

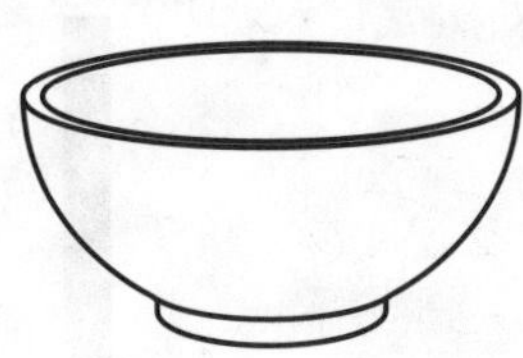

DIRECTIONS 1–6. Compare the capacity of each container. Circle the container that holds more. Mark an X on the container that holds less.

Lesson Check

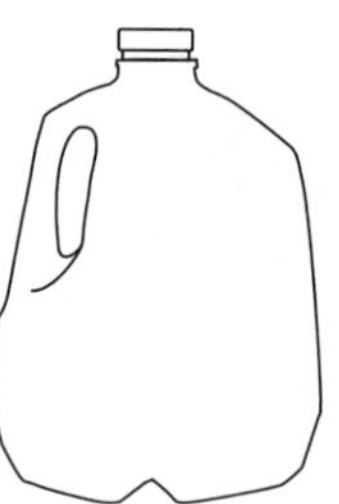

Spiral Review

8 5

6

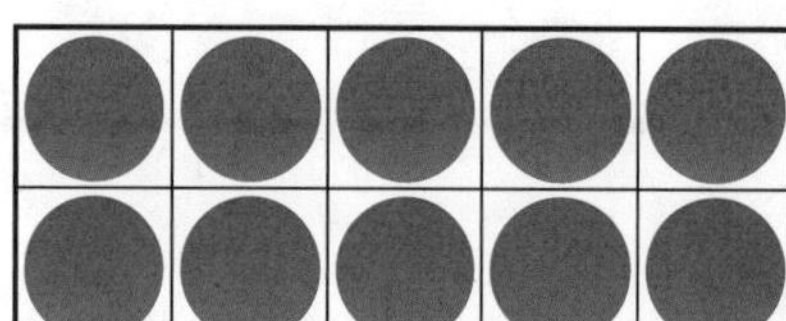

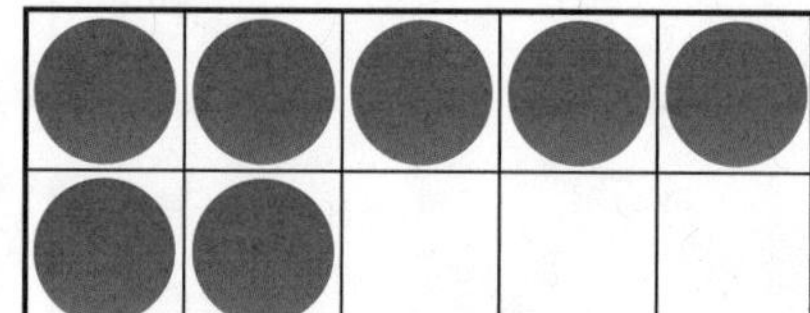

7 10 17

DIRECTIONS 1–2. Compare the capacity of each container. Circle the container that holds more. Mark an X on the container that holds less. **3.** Circle the greater number. **4.** Look at the number. Write the number that is one more. **5.** How many counters? Circle the number.

Name ______________________________

Explore Temperature

Essential Question How can you identify the difference between warm and cool temperatures?

Learning Objective You will identify the difference between warm and cool temperatures.

Listen and Draw Real World

DIRECTIONS Chloe was looking at magazine pictures to decide on a vacation. Trace the circle on the picture that shows a warm place. Trace the X on the picture that shows a cool place. Tell a friend what clues in each picture helped you decide which was a warm place and which was a cool place.

Share and Show

4

5

6

DIRECTIONS 1–6. Look at each picture. Circle the picture in red if it most likely shows a warm temperature. Circle the picture in blue if it most likely shows a cool temperature. Tell a friend how you know.

Name ______________________________

7

8

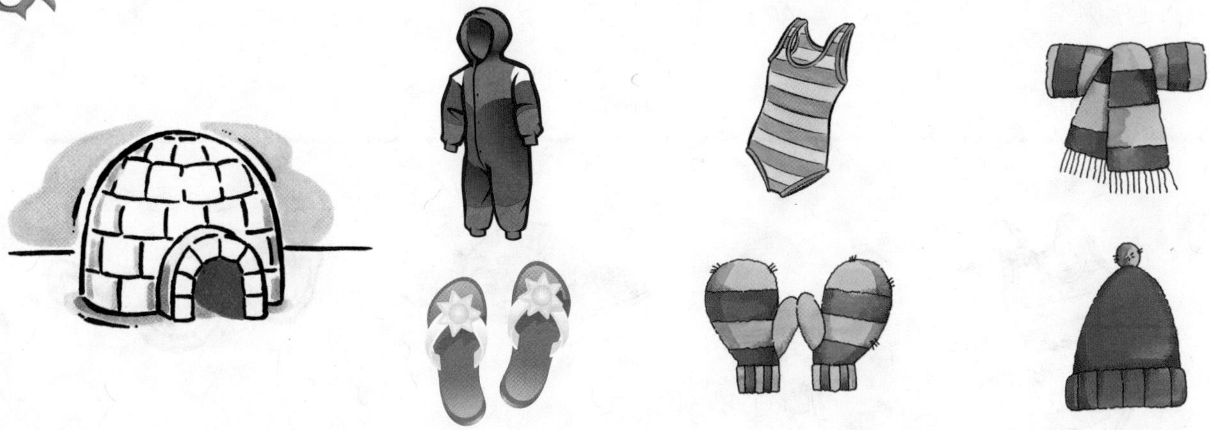

9

DIRECTIONS 7–9. Look at the picture. Circle the clothing you would most likely wear to play if you were there. Tell a friend how you know.

Problem Solving • Applications Real World

WRITE Math

10

11

DIRECTIONS 10. Malik picked out these clothes to go outside and play. Draw a picture of where he might go and what he might be doing there. 11. Camila picked out these clothes to go outside and play. Draw a picture of where she might go and what she might be doing there.

HOME CONNECTION • Ask your child what activity he or she might do in a warm temperature. Then have your child show what clothing he or she would wear for the activity. Repeat for a cool temperature.

Name ________________________________

Explore Temperature

Learning Objective You will identify the difference between warm and cool temperatures.

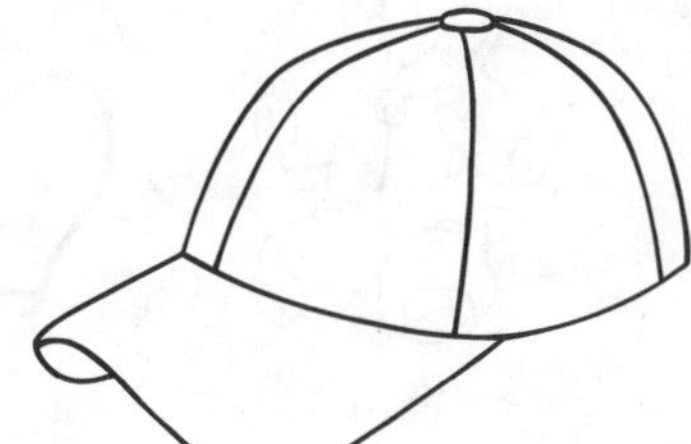

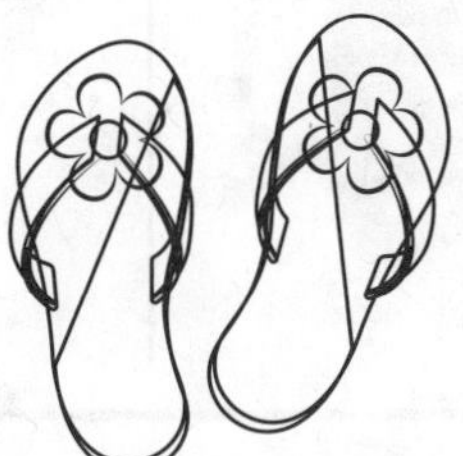

DIRECTIONS 1–4. Look at the picture. Color the clothing that you would most likely wear to play if you were there. Tell how you know.

Lesson Check

1

2

3

Spiral Review

4

5

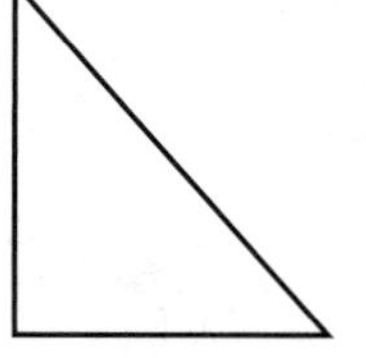

______ sides

DIRECTIONS 1–2. Look at the picture. Circle the picture in red if it most likely shows a warm temperature. Circle the picture in blue if it most likely shows a cool temperature. **3.** Look at the picture. Color the clothing that you would most likely wear to play if you were there. **4.** Circle the container that holds more. Mark an X on the container that holds less. **5.** How many sides does the shape have? Write the number.

Name ______________________________

Temperature

Essential Question How can you compare the temperatures of warm and cool objects?

Learning Objective You will compare the temperatures of warm and cool objects.

Listen and Draw Real World

DIRECTIONS Look at the pictures. Trace the circle on the picture that shows a warm temperature. Trace the X on the picture that shows a cool temperature.

Share and Show

2

DIRECTIONS 1. Trace the circle around the picture that shows a warmer temperature than the first picture in the row. **2–3.** Circle the picture that shows something warmer than the first picture in the row.

Name ___________________________________

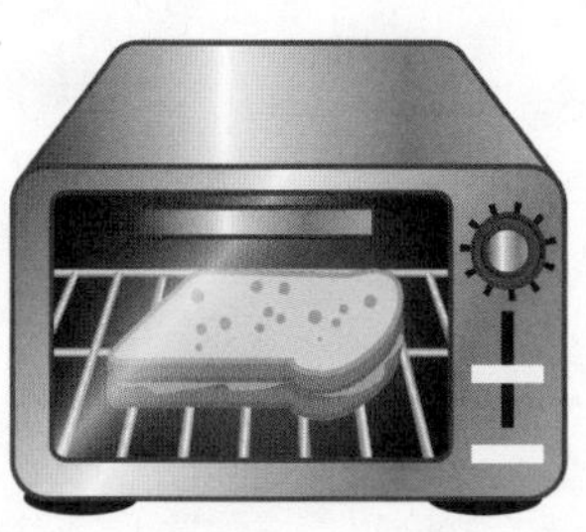

DIRECTIONS 4–6. Circle the picture that shows something cooler than the first picture in the row.

Problem Solving • Applications Real World

WRITE Math

7

8

DIRECTIONS 7. Draw to show an object you may use in a cool temperature. **8.** Draw to show an object you may use in a warm temperature.

HOME CONNECTION • Ask your child to name a favorite object he or she may use in a warm temperature. Then repeat for a favorite object he or she may use in a cool temperature.

Name ______________________________

Temperature

Learning Objective You will compare the temperatures of warm and cool objects.

DIRECTIONS 1–4. Use blue to color the cool objects. Use red to color the warm objects.

Lesson Check

Spiral Review

before 10 o'clock

about 10 o'clock

after 10 o'clock

DIRECTIONS 1–2. Use red to color the warm object. Use blue to color the cool object. 3. Circle the time shown on the clock. 4. Mark an X on the cylinder that is far from the cone. Draw a circle around the cylinder that is between the cone and the cube.

Name ______________________________

Morning, Afternoon, and Evening

Essential Question How can you understand time such as morning, afternoon, and evening?

Learning Objective You will understand time such as morning, afternoon, and evening.

Listen and Draw Real World

morning

afternoon

evening

morning

afternoon

evening

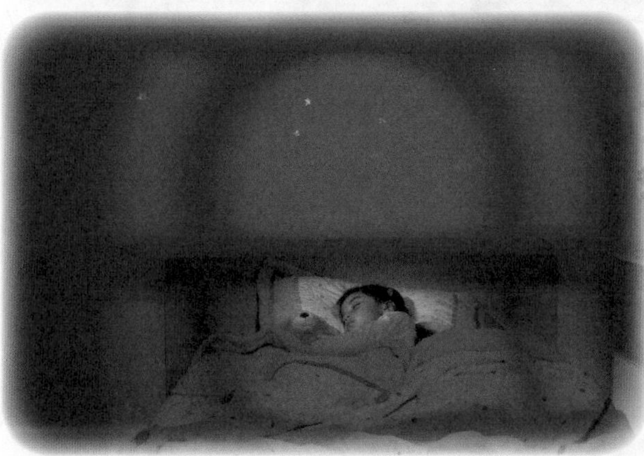

morning

afternoon

evening

DIRECTIONS Look at the pictures. Talk about what is happening in the pictures. Trace the circle around the time of day when this activity may take place.

Share and Show

DIRECTIONS 1. Trace the circle around the picture that shows the morning. 2. Circle the picture that shows the evening.

Name ______________________________

DIRECTIONS 3. Circle the picture that shows the morning. 4. Circle the picture that shows the afternoon.

Problem Solving • Applications

5

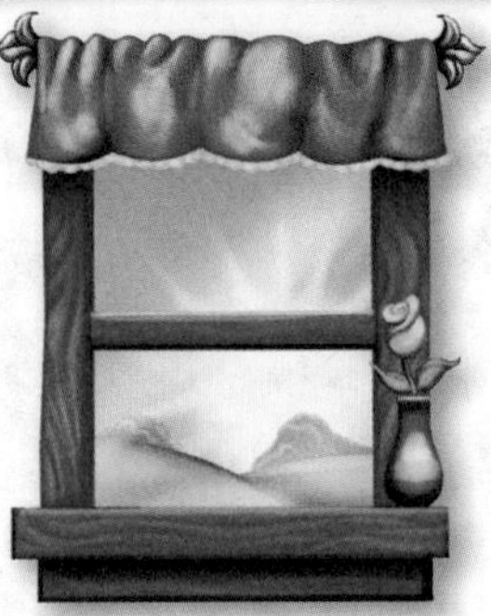

morning

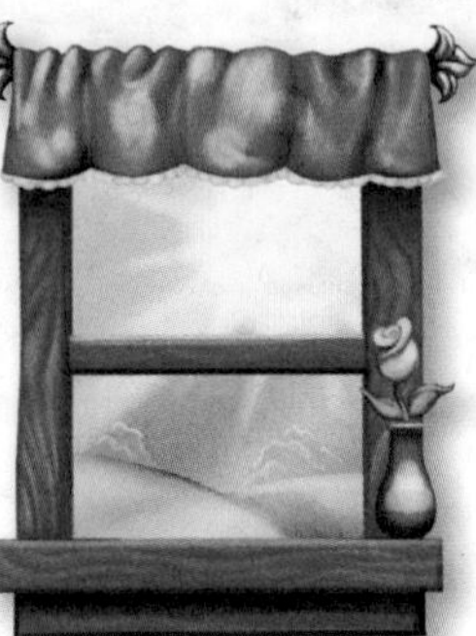

afternoon

evening

DIRECTIONS 5–7. Draw to show what you know about morning, afternoon, and evening.

HOME ACTIVITY • Have your child draw three pictures to show how he or she understands morning, afternoon, and evening.

Name ______________________________

Morning, Afternoon, and Evening

Learning Objective You will understand time such as *morning*, *afternoon*, and *evening.*

1

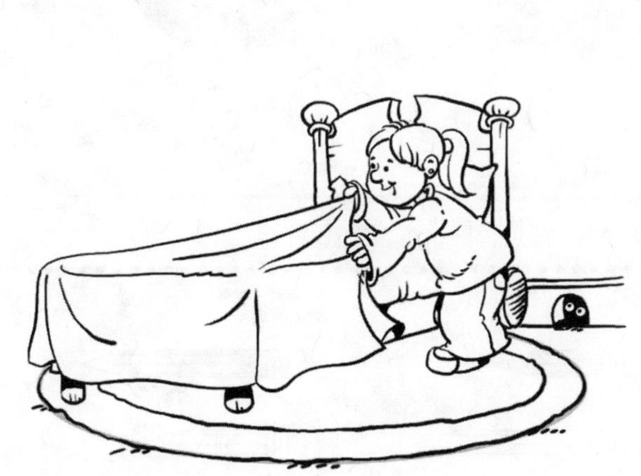

DIRECTIONS 1. Circle the picture that shows the morning.
2. Circle the picture that shows the afternoon.

Lesson Check

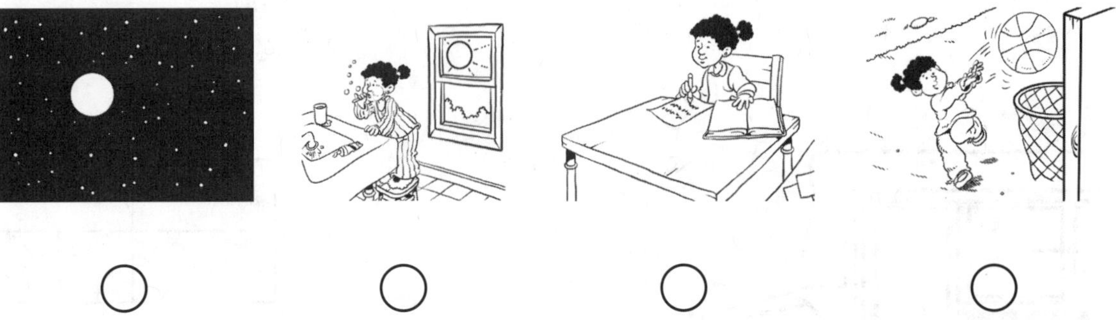

Spiral Review

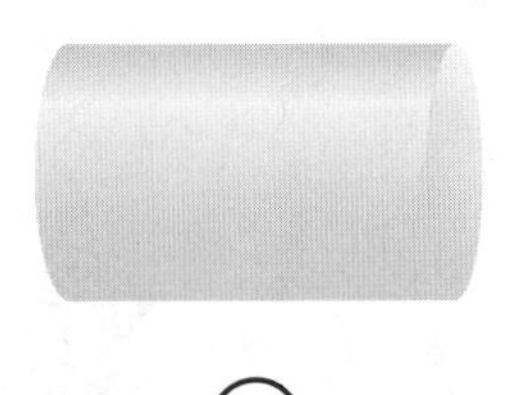

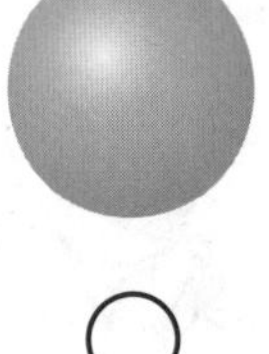

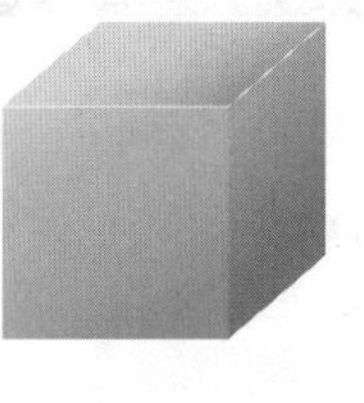

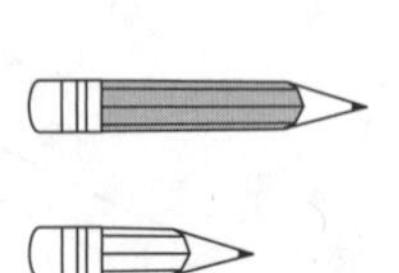

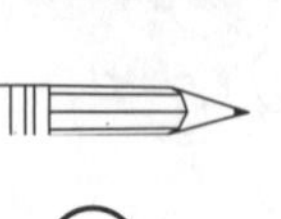

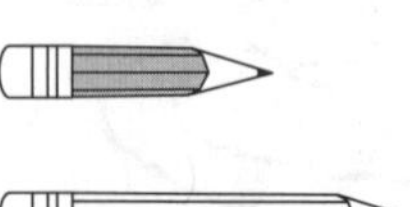

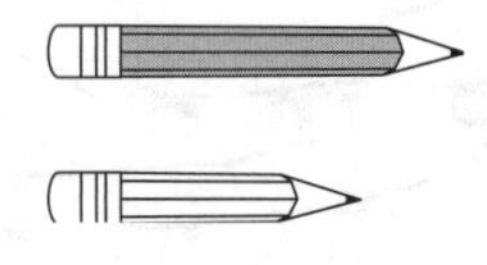

DIRECTIONS 1. Which picture shows the evening? Mark your answer. **2.** What shape is the orange? Mark under your answer. **3.** Which picture shows the gray pencil shorter than the white pencil? Mark under your answer

Name ____

Days in a Week

Essential Question How can you understand time such as the days in a week?

Learning Objective You will understand time such as the days in a week.

Listen and Draw Real World

DIRECTIONS Point to each day name as you say them in order. Circle the name for today. Draw something you would like to do today.

Share and Show

1

Sunday	Monday	Tuesday	Wednesday	Thursday	Friday	Saturday

2

Tuesday	
Friday	
Sunday	1
Wednesday	
Saturday	
Monday	
Thursday	

DIRECTIONS 1. Point to and say each day of the week. Circle the name for today. 2. Number the days in order, beginning with Sunday.

Name ______________________________

Sunday	Monday	Tuesday	Wednesday	Thursday	Friday	Saturday

1 2 3

fishing swimming soccer

5

Monday Tuesday Friday

DIRECTIONS Circle your answer. **3.** On how many days is soccer played? **4.** Which sport is played on Wednesday? **5.** On which day is the piano lesson?

Problem Solving • Applications

WRITE Math

6

5 6 7 days in a week

7

Monday Wednesday Friday

8

Thursday Saturday Tuesday

DIRECTIONS Circle your answer.
6. How many days are in a week?
7. Which day is two days after Wednesday?
8. Which day is one week from Saturday?

HOME ACTIVITY • Have your child say the days of the week in order beginning with Sunday.

Name ______________________________

Days in a Week

Learning Objective You will understand time such as the days in a week.

Sunday	Monday	Tuesday	Wednesday	Thursday	Friday	Saturday
		Paint		Paint		

1 2 3

basketball art class soccer

Monday Tuesday Wednesday

DIRECTIONS Circle your answer. **1.** On how many days is there an art class? **2.** What happens on Sunday? **3.** On which day is the violin lesson?

Lesson Check

Sunday Monday Tuesday Wednesday Thursday Friday Saturday

Monday ○ Tuesday ○ Wednesday ○ Thursday ○

Spiral Review

1 ○ 2 ○ 3 ○ 4 ○

3

4

DIRECTIONS 1. Which day is three days after Monday? Mark under your answer. **2.** How many vertices does the square have? Mark under your answer. **3.** Look at the cube train. Draw a train that is taller than this one. **4.** Draw a star outside of the rectangle.

Name ____________________

Today, Yesterday, Tomorrow

Essential Question How can you understand time such as today, yesterday, and tomorrow?

Learning Objective You will understand time such as today, yesterday, and tomorrow.

Yesterday	Today	Tomorrow

Sunday	Monday	Tuesday	Wednesday	Thursday	Friday	Saturday

DIRECTIONS Look at the charts. Find the days that are yesterday, today, and tomorrow.

Share and Show

1

DIRECTIONS 1. Find the name of the day it is today. Trace the name. Draw a line to the word *today*. Do the same for the name of the day before today and the word *yesterday*. Do the same for the name of the day after today and the word *tomorrow*.

Name ________________________________

DIRECTIONS 2. Draw something that happened yesterday. 3. Draw something that is happening today. 4. Draw something that may happen tomorrow.

Problem Solving • Applications

5

6

DIRECTIONS 5. Today is Thursday. Maya plays piano on Wednesday. She plays soccer on Friday. What will she do tomorrow? Circle your answer. 6. Today is Sunday. Bobby will bake tomorrow. He read a book yesterday. What does he do on Monday? Circle your answer.

HOME ACTIVITY • Have your child tell you what day it was yesterday.

Name ______________________________

Today, Yesterday, Tomorrow

Learning Objective You will understand time such as today, yesterday, and tomorrow.

yesterday

today

tomorrow

DIRECTIONS 1. Draw something that happened yesterday. **2.** Draw something that is happening today. **3.** Draw something that may happen tomorrow.

Lesson Check

Sunday	Monday	Tuesday	Wednesday	Thursday	Friday	Saturday

Sunday ○ Tuesday ○ Wednesday ○ Thursday ○

Spiral Review

○ ○ ○ ○

DIRECTIONS 1. If today is Monday, what day will it be tomorrow? Mark under your answer. **2.** Which object is heavier than the book? Circle your answer. **3.** Which shape is a cube? Mark under your answer.

Name ______________________________

Weeks in a Month

Essential Question How can you understand time such as the weeks in a month?

Learning Objective You will understand time such as the weeks in a month.

Listen and Draw (Real World)

May

Sunday	Monday	Tuesday	Wednesday	Thursday	Friday	Saturday
1	2	3	4	5	6	7
8	9	10	11	12	13	14
15	16	17	18	19	20	21
22	23	24	25	26	27	28
29	30	31				

DIRECTIONS Look at the calendar. Point to each date as you count. Talk about the days in a week and the full weeks in this month. Color the second week of this month.

Share and Show

August

Sunday	Monday	Tuesday	Wednesday	Thursday	Friday	Saturday
	1	2	3	4	5	6
7	8	9	10	11	12	13
14	15	16	17	18	19	20
21	22	23	24	25	26	27
28	29	30	31			

1.
4
5
6

2.
4
5
6

3. ✓
Sunday
Monday
Tuesday

4. ✓
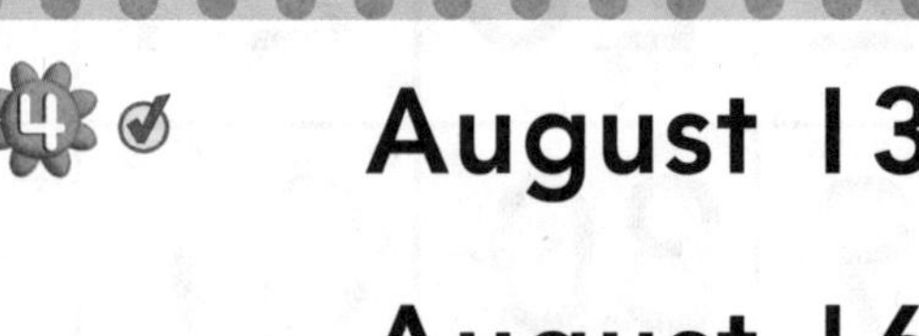
August 13
August 16
August 19

DIRECTIONS Look at the calendar. Circle your answer. **1.** How many Mondays are in this month? **2.** How many Fridays are in this month? **3.** What day of the week is August 9? **4.** What date is one week after August 9?

Name ________________________________

5

November

Sunday	Monday	Tuesday	Wednesday	Thursday	Friday	Saturday
		1	2	3	4	5
6	7	8	9	10	11	12
13	14	15	16	17	18	19
20	21	22	23	24	25	26
27	28	29	30			

DIRECTIONS 5. Use red to color the name of the month. Use yellow to color the names of the days of the week. Use green to color the third week of the month. Use blue to color the fourth week of the month.

Problem Solving • Applications

WRITE Math

6

November

Sunday	Monday	Tuesday	Wednesday	Thursday	Friday	Saturday
		1	2	3	4	5
6	7	8	9	10	11	12
13	14	15	16	17	18	19
20	21	22	23	24	25	26
27	28	29	30			

December

Sunday	Monday	Tuesday	Wednesday	Thursday	Friday	Saturday
				1	2	3
4	5	6	7	8	9	10
11	12	13	14	15	16	17
18	19	20	21	22	23	24
25	26	27	28	29	30	31

Sunday Monday Tuesday Wednesday

Thursday Friday Saturday

DIRECTIONS 6. If the last day of the month is Wednesday, what will be the first day of the next month? Circle that day. 7. Draw to show an activity you like to do in one of these months.

HOME ACTIVITY • Have your child tell you what day of the week it will be one week from today.

Name ______________________

Weeks in a Month

Learning Objective You will understand time such as the weeks in a month.

September

Sunday	Monday	Tuesday	Wednesday	Thursday	Friday	Saturday
		1	2	3	4	5
6	7	8	9	10	11	12
13	14	15	16	17	18	19
20	21	22	23	24	25	26
27	28	29	30			

DIRECTIONS 1. Use orange to color the name of the month. Use red to color the names of the days of the week. Use yellow to color the second week of the month. Use green to color the fourth week of the month.

Lesson Check

MAY						
Sunday	Monday	Tuesday	Wednesday	Thursday	Friday	Saturday
1	2	3	4	5	6	7

Sunday ○ Monday ○ Tuesday ○ Wednesday ○

Spiral Review

2

○ ○ ○ ○

3

○ ○ ○ ○

DIRECTIONS 1. What day is the third day of May? Mark under your answer. **2.** Which basket shows a piece of fruit inside the basket? Mark under your answer. **3.** Count and tell how many cubes are in the cube train. Write the number. Mark under the cube train that is longer.

Name ______________________________

Months in a Year

Essential Question How can you understand time such as the months in a year?

Learning Objective You will understand time such as months in a year.

Listen and Draw Real World

January

Sunday	Monday	Tuesday	Wednesday	Thursday	Friday	Saturday
					1	2
3	4	5	6	7	8	9
10	11	12	13	14	15	16
17	18	19	20	21	22	23
24	25	26	27	28	29	30
31						

February

Sunday	Monday	Tuesday	Wednesday	Thursday	Friday	Saturday
	1	2	3	4	5	6
7	8	9	10	11	12	13
14	15	16	17	18	19	20
21	22	23	24	25	26	27
28						

March

Sunday	Monday	Tuesday	Wednesday	Thursday	Friday	Saturday
	1	2	3	4	5	6
7	8	9	10	11	12	13
14	15	16	17	18	19	20
21	22	23	24	25	26	27
28	29	30	31			

April

Sunday	Monday	Tuesday	Wednesday	Thursday	Friday	Saturday
				1	2	3
4	5	6	7	8	9	10
11	12	13	14	15	16	17
18	19	20	21	22	23	24
25	26	27	28	29	30	

May

Sunday	Monday	Tuesday	Wednesday	Thursday	Friday	Saturday
						1
2	3	4	5	6	7	8
9	10	11	12	13	14	15
16	17	18	19	20	21	22
23	24	25	26	27	28	29
30	31					

June

Sunday	Monday	Tuesday	Wednesday	Thursday	Friday	Saturday
		1	2	3	4	5
6	7	8	9	10	11	12
13	14	15	16	17	18	19
20	21	22	23	24	25	26
27	28	29	30			

July

Sunday	Monday	Tuesday	Wednesday	Thursday	Friday	Saturday
				1	2	3
4	5	6	7	8	9	10
11	12	13	14	15	16	17
18	19	20	21	22	23	24
25	26	27	28	29	30	31

August

Sunday	Monday	Tuesday	Wednesday	Thursday	Friday	Saturday
1	2	3	4	5	6	7
8	9	10	11	12	13	14
15	16	17	18	19	20	21
22	23	24	25	26	27	28
29	30	31				

September

Sunday	Monday	Tuesday	Wednesday	Thursday	Friday	Saturday
			1	2	3	4
5	6	7	8	9	10	11
12	13	14	15	16	17	18
19	20	21	22	23	24	25
26	27	28	29	30		

October

Sunday	Monday	Tuesday	Wednesday	Thursday	Friday	Saturday
					1	2
3	4	5	6	7	8	9
10	11	12	13	14	15	16
17	18	19	20	21	22	23
24	25	26	27	28	29	30
31						

November

Sunday	Monday	Tuesday	Wednesday	Thursday	Friday	Saturday
	1	2	3	4	5	6
7	8	9	10	11	12	13
14	15	16	17	18	19	20
21	22	23	24	25	26	27
28	29	30				

December

Sunday	Monday	Tuesday	Wednesday	Thursday	Friday	Saturday
			1	2	3	4
5	6	7	8	9	10	11
12	13	14	15	16	17	18
19	20	21	22	23	24	25
26	27	28	29	30	31	

DIRECTIONS Point to the months as you say them in order. Count to find out how many months are in one year. Circle the month it is now.

Share and Show

January	February	March	April	May	June

January February March

April May June

DIRECTIONS 1. Trace the circle around the month that comes between January and March. 2. Circle the month that comes after May.

Name ___________________________________

July	August	September	October	November	December

July August September

October November December

DIRECTIONS 3. Circle the month that comes between July and September. 4. Circle the month that comes before November.

Problem Solving • Applications Real World

January	
February	
March	
April	
May	
June	
July	
August	
September	
October	
November	
December	

WRITE Math

5
February
March
May

6
July
November
January

7
12
10
14

8
April
June
July

DIRECTIONS Circle your answer.
5. What month comes right before April?
6. What is the first month of the year?
7. How many months are in one year?
8. What month comes right after May?

HOME ACTIVITY • Show your child a year calendar. Have your child name the months of the year as he or she points to them.

Name ____________________

Months in a Year

Learning Objective You will understand time using months in a year.

January	February	March	April	May	June

January February March

April May June

DIRECTIONS 1. Circle the month that comes before February.
2. Circle the month that comes between April and June.

Lesson Check

January February ________

December March April May

○ ○ ○ ○

September November August

○ ○ ○

Spiral Review

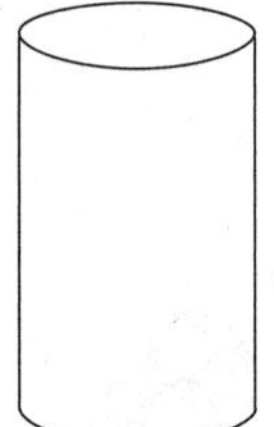

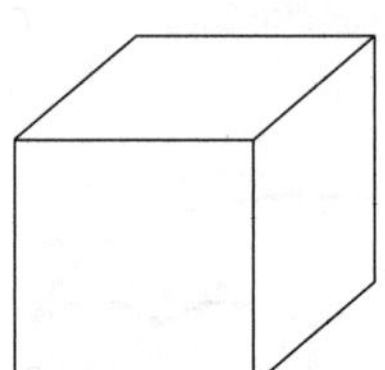

7 8 9 10

○ ○ ○ ○

DIRECTIONS 1. Which month comes after February? Mark under your answer. 2. Which month comes right before October? Mark under your answer. 3. Which shape is a cylinder? Circle the shape. 4. How many cherries are left? Mark under your answer.

Name ______________________________

Use a Clock

Essential Question How can you use the hour hand on a clock to tell about what time it is?

Learning Objective You will learn how to use the hour hand on a clock to tell about what time it is.

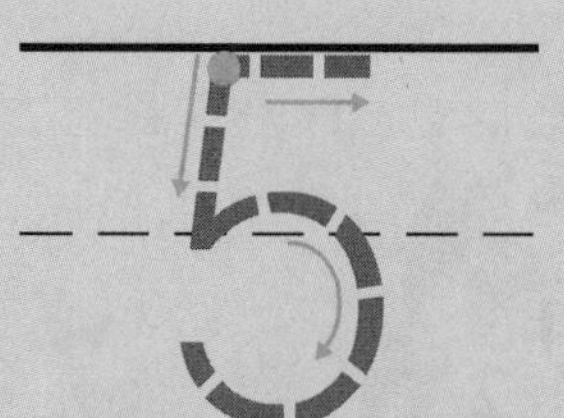

About ______ o'clock

About ______ o'clock

DIRECTIONS 1. Jayden looked at the hour hand on her clock. It was pointing to the 5. About what time is it? Trace the number. 2. Ava looked at the hour hand on her clock. It was pointing to the 9. About what time is it? Write the number.

Share and Show

before 2 o'clock

about 2 o'clock

after 2 o'clock

before 7 o'clock

about 7 o'clock

after 7 o'clock

before 11 o'clock

about 11 o'clock

after 11 o'clock

DIRECTIONS 3–5. Circle the time that the watch shows.

Name ______________________________

before 8 o'clock

about 8 o'clock

after 8 o'clock

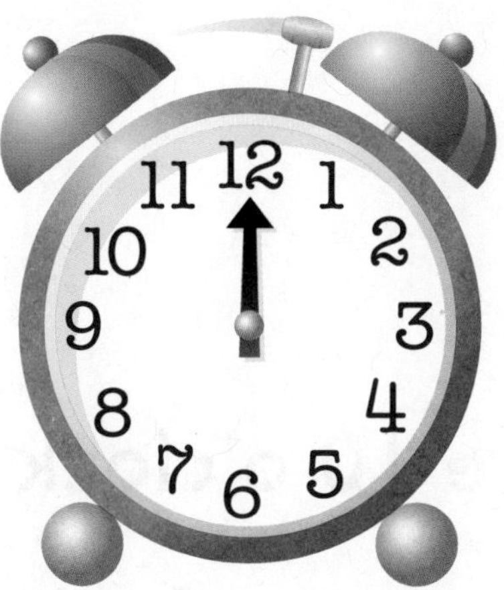

before 12 o'clock

about 12 o'clock

after 12 o'clock

before 4 o'clock

about 4 o'clock

after 4 o'clock

DIRECTIONS 6–8. Circle the time that the clock shows.

Problem Solving • Applications Real World

9

10

before 10 o'clock

about 10 o'clock

after 10 o'clock

DIRECTIONS 9. Ichara looked at her alarm clock. She saw it was after 7 o'clock. Circle the clock she was reading. 10. Isabella's mom asks her, "What time does the clock show?" Look at the clock and circle the time Isabella sees.

HOME CONNECTION • Draw a simple clock with just 12 numbers and no hands or minute marks. Ask your child where the hour hand should be to show about 3 o'clock, after 6 o'clock, before 2 o'clock. You can provide a toothpick to have your child place the hour hand where it belongs.

Name ________________________________

Use a Clock

Learning Objective You will learn how to use the hour hand on a clock to tell about what time it is.

before 3 o'clock

about 3 o'clock

after 3 o'clock

before 6 o'clock

about 6 o'clock

after 6 o'clock

before 1 o'clock

about 1 o'clock

after 1 o'clock

DIRECTIONS 1–3. Circle the time that the clock shows.

Lesson Check

before 7 o'clock

about 7 o'clock

after 7 o'clock

before 5 o'clock

about 5 o'clock

after 5 o'clock

Spiral Review

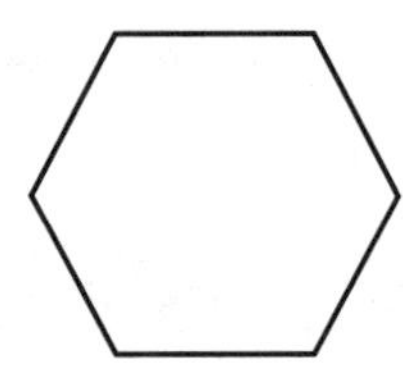

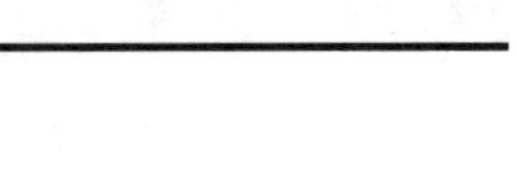

sides

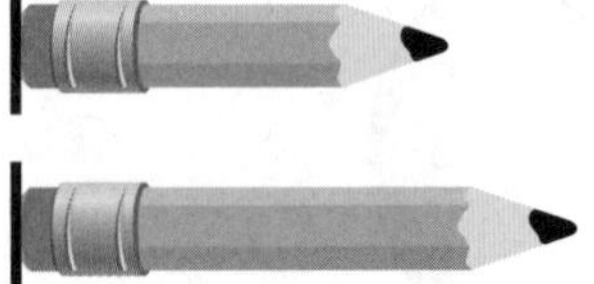

DIRECTIONS 1–2. Circle the time that the clock shows.
3. How many sides does the hexagon have? Write the number.
4. Look at pencils. Circle the pencil that is shorter.

Name ______________________________

Problem Solving • More Concrete Graphs

Essential Question How can you solve problems by using the strategy *make a graph*?

Learning Objective You will use the strategy *make a graph* to solve problems.

Unlock the Problem

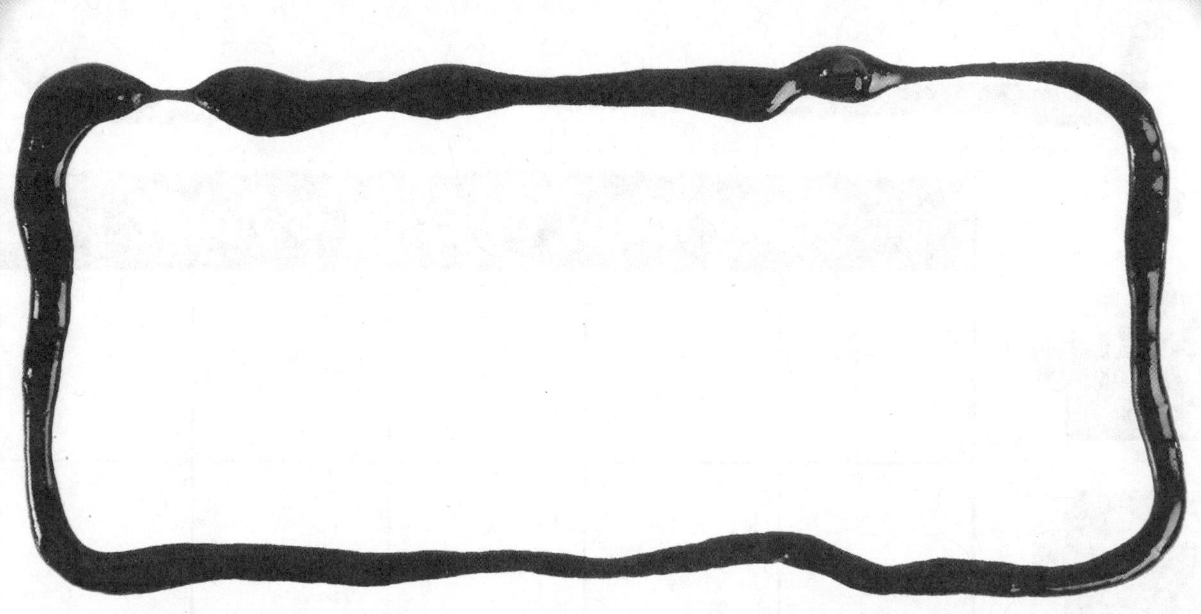

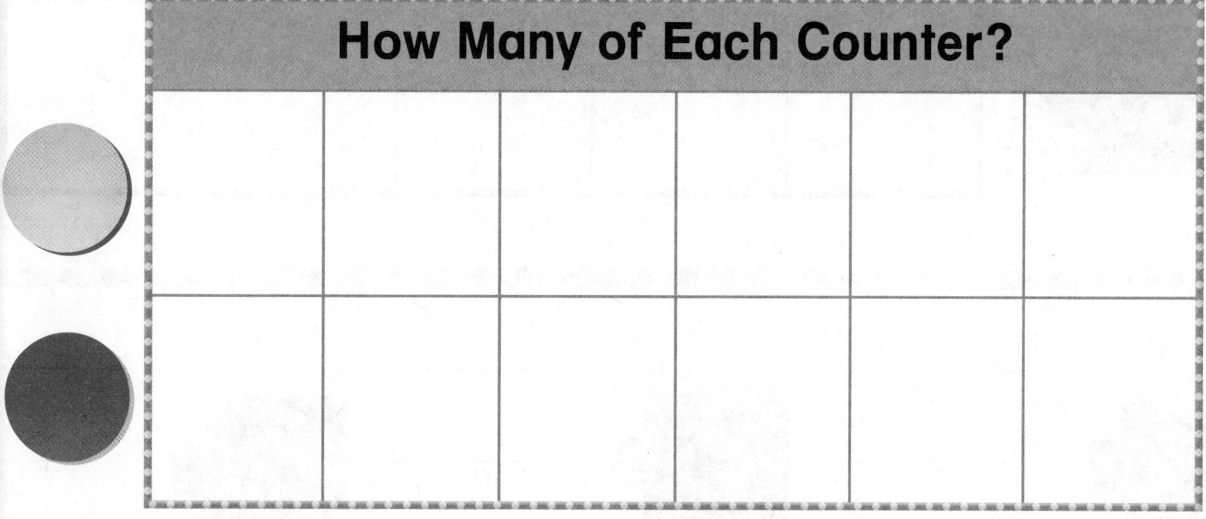

DIRECTIONS Place a handful of counters on the workspace. Sort the counters. Tell a friend how you sorted the counters. Move the counters to the graph. Draw and color the counters. Tell a friend about the graph.

Try Another Problem

1

2

How Many of Each Color?				

3

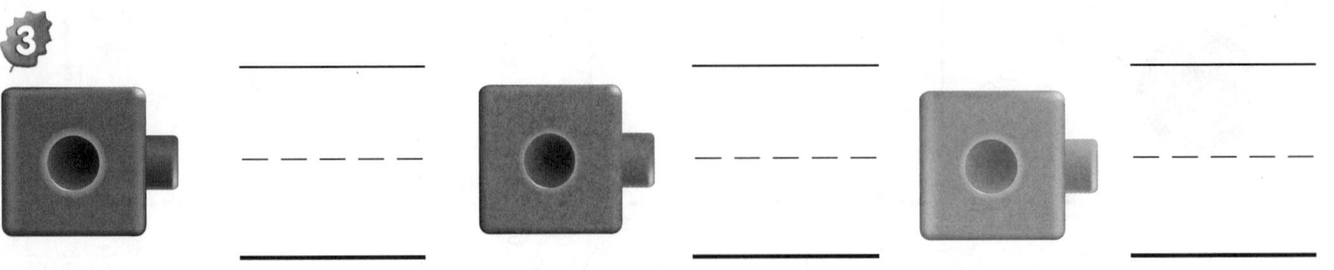

DIRECTIONS 1. Place a handful of red, blue, and green cubes on the workspace. Sort the cubes. 2. Move the cubes to the graph. Draw and color the cubes. 3. Write how many of each cube. Which color shows the fewest cubes? Circle that cube.

Name ____________________

Share and Show

4

5

How Many of Each Shape?						
circle						
square						
triangle						

6

DIRECTIONS 4. Place a handful of small green shapes on the workspace. Sort the shapes. 5. Move the shapes to the graph. Draw and color the shapes. 6. Write how many of each shape. Which has the most shapes? Circle that shape.

On Your Own

7

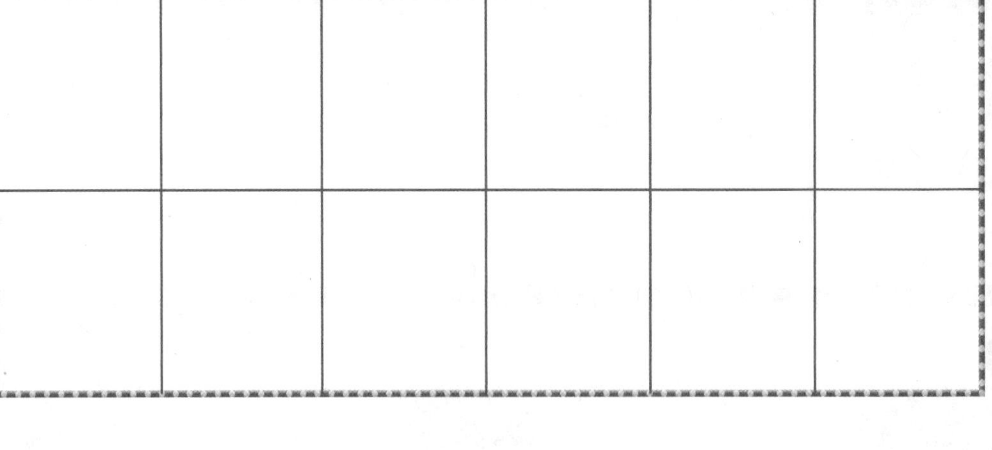

DIRECTIONS 7. There are three red cubes. There are two more blue cubes than red cubes. Draw to show the cubes on the graph. **8.** Use five cubes of two colors. Draw and color to show what you know about making a graph with those cubes.

HOME ACTIVITY • Have your child tell about the graph that he or she made on this page. Ask your child which row has more counters and which row has fewer counters.

Name ______________________________

Problem Solving • More Concrete Graphs

Learning Objective You will use the strategy *make a graph* to solve problems.

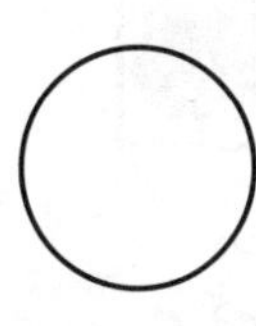

How Many of Each Shape?				

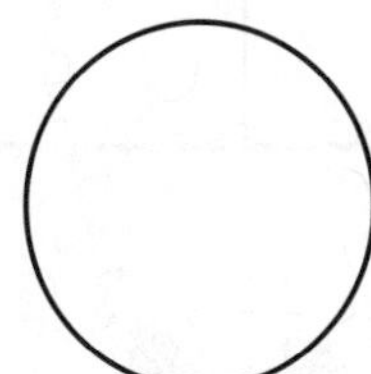

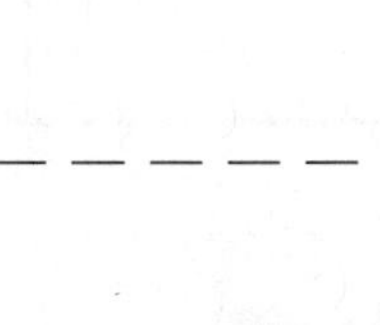

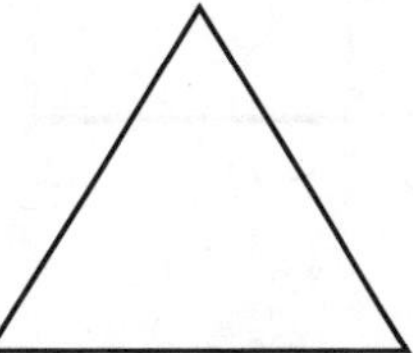

DIRECTIONS 1. Place a handful of small green circles and triangles on the workspace. Sort the shapes. 2. Move the shapes to the graph. Draw and color the shapes. 3. Write how many of each shape. Which has the fewest shapes? Circle that shape.

Lesson Check

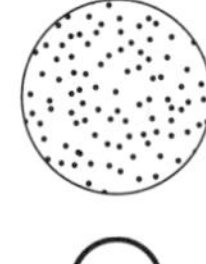

Spiral Review

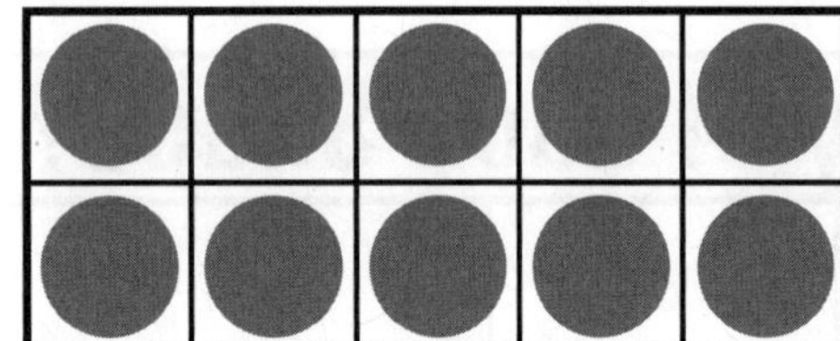
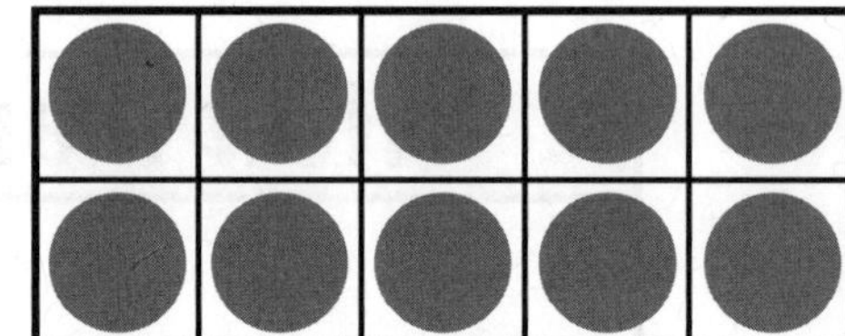

17 18 19 20

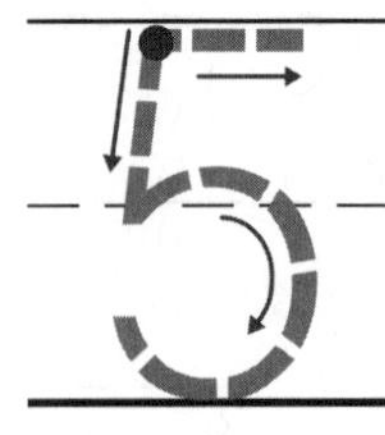

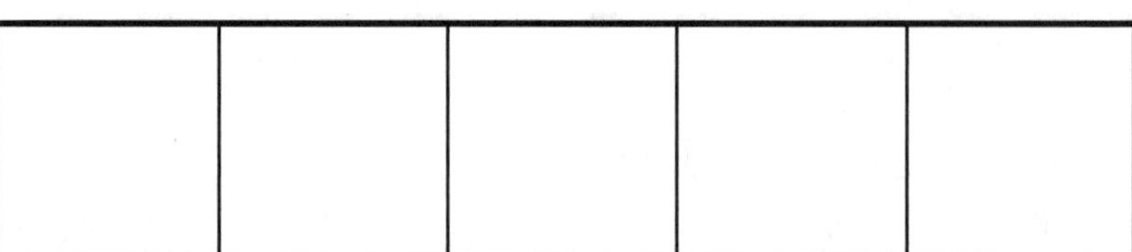

DIRECTIONS **1.** Which row has more counters? Mark under your answer. **2.** How many counters? Mark under your answer. **3.** Trace the number. How many counters would you place in the five frame? Circle your answer.

Name ______________________________

Algebra: Describe and Copy a Shape Pattern

Essential Question How can you describe and copy a shape pattern?

Learning Objective You will describe and copy a shape pattern.

Listen and Draw

DIRECTIONS Point to each shape as you describe the pattern. Which part of the pattern repeats again and again? Use shapes to copy the pattern. Trace the shapes.

Share and Show

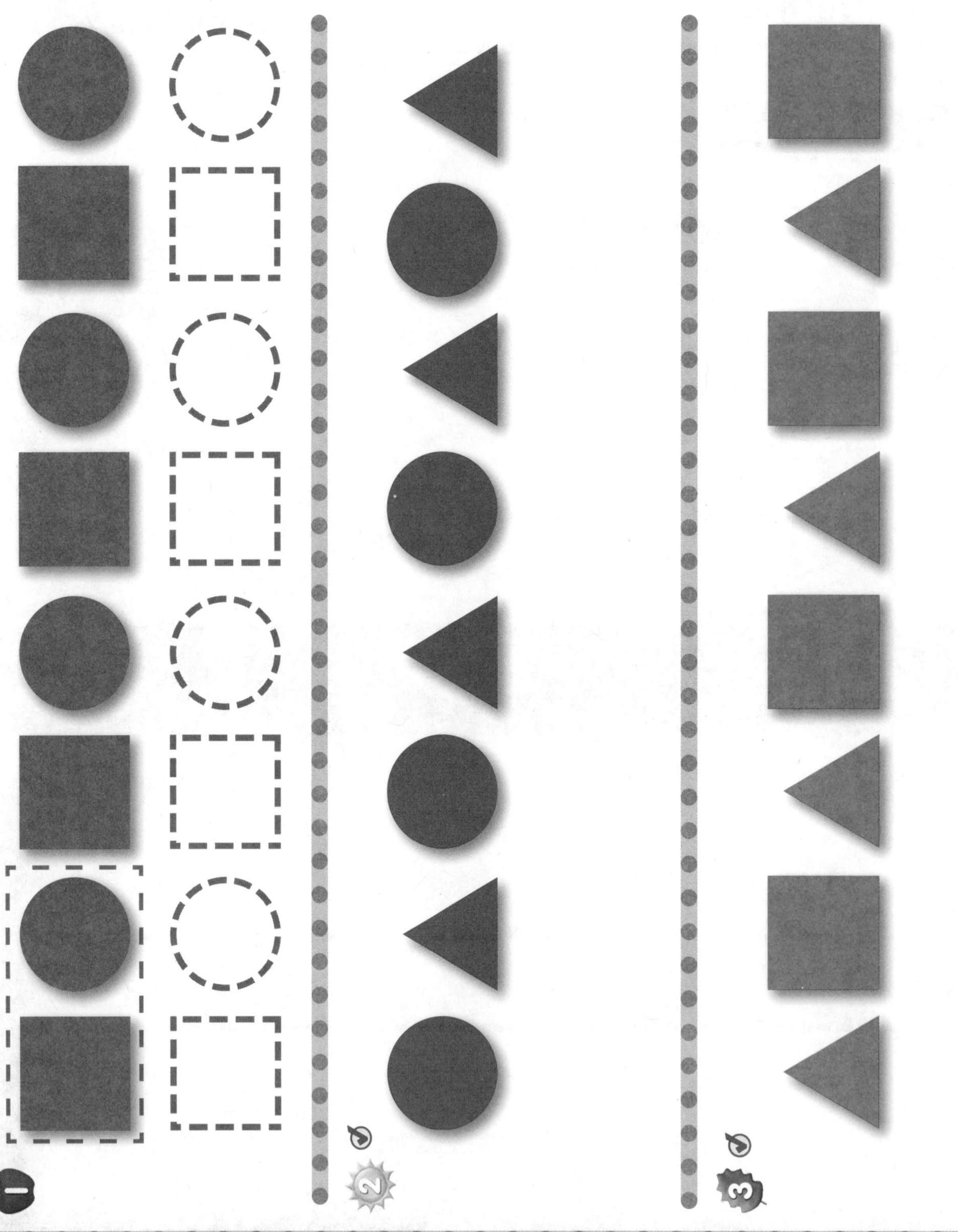

DIRECTIONS Read to describe the pattern. Which part of the pattern repeats again and again? **1.** Trace the box around that part. Place shapes to copy the pattern. Trace the pattern. **2–3.** Draw a box around the part of the pattern that repeats. Place shapes to copy the pattern. Draw and color the pattern.

Name ______________________________

4

5

6

DIRECTIONS 4–6. Read to describe the pattern. Which part of the pattern repeats again and again? Draw a box around that part. Place shapes to copy the pattern. Draw and color the pattern.

Problem Solving • Applications Real World

7

WRITE Math

8

DIRECTIONS 7. Which shape is missing in the pattern? Draw and color the shape where it belongs. Draw a box around the part of the pattern that repeats again and again. **8.** Draw and color to show what you know about a shape pattern.

HOME ACTIVITY • Have your child use household objects to show you a shape pattern.

Name ______________________________

Algebra: Describe and Copy a Shape Pattern

Learning Objective You will describe and copy a shape pattern.

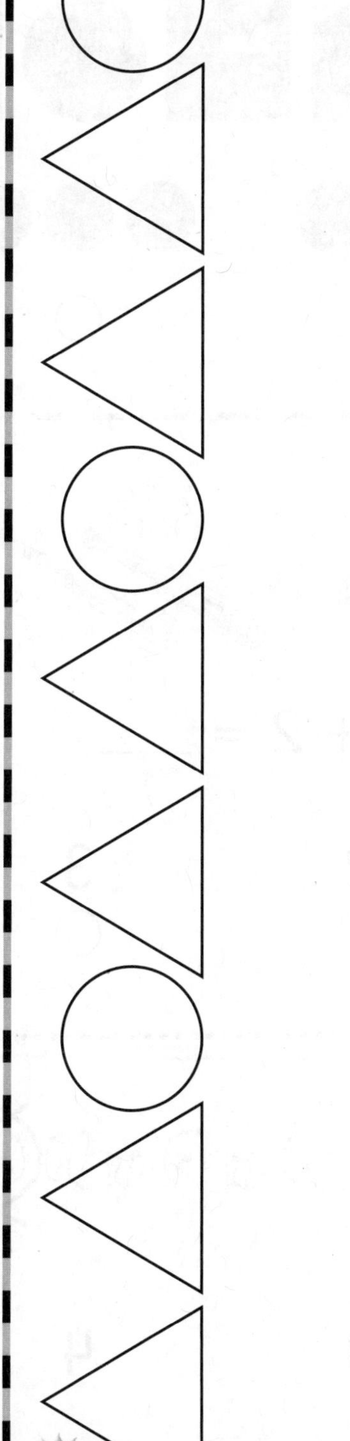

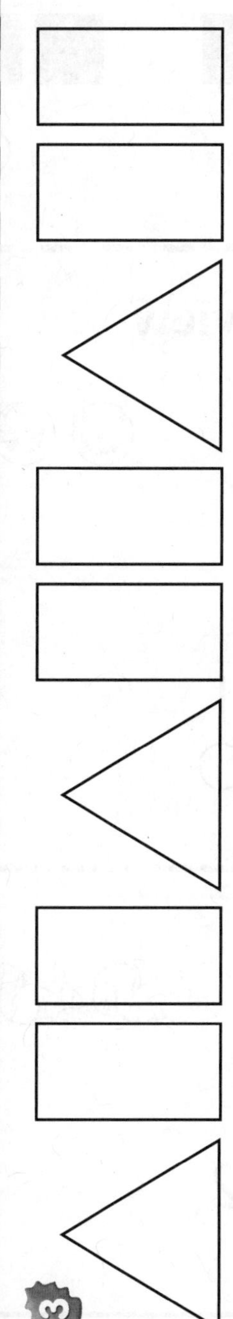

1

2

3

DIRECTIONS 1–3. Read to describe the pattern. Which part of the pattern repeats again and again? Draw a box around that part. Place shapes to copy the pattern. Draw and color the pattern.

Lesson Check

Spiral Review

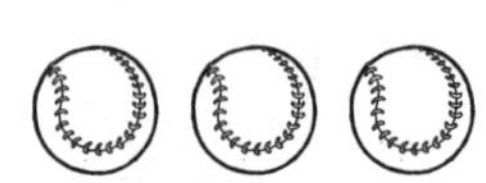 

3 + 2 = ___

1 2 3 5

2 3 4 5

DIRECTIONS 1. Which set of shapes shows the pattern? Mark under your answer. 2. How many objects in all? Mark under your answer. 3. How many squirrels are left? Circle your answer.

Name ______________________________

Algebra: Extend a Shape Pattern

Essential Question How can you extend a shape pattern?

Learning Objective You will extend a shape pattern.

Listen and Draw

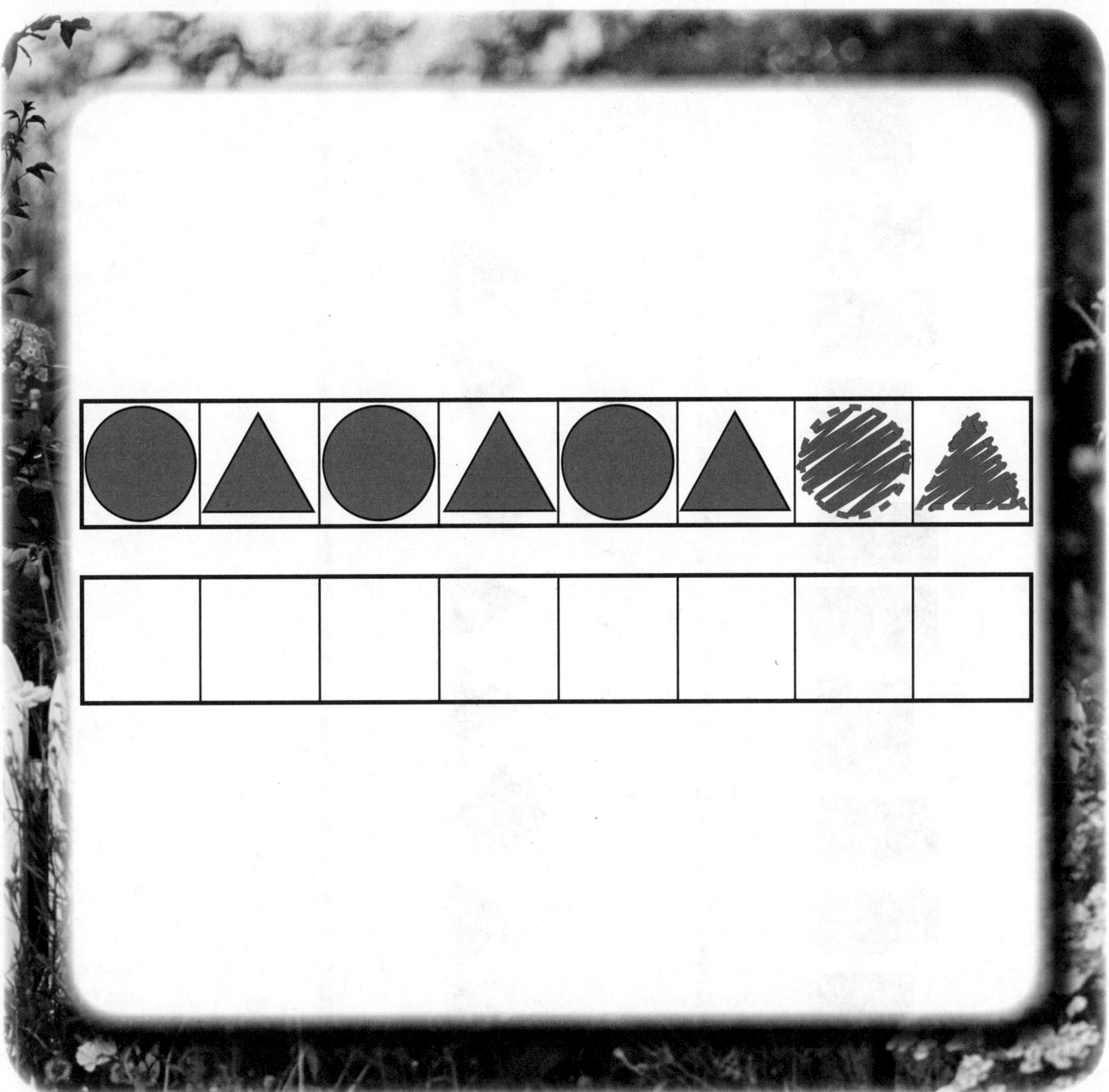

DIRECTIONS Place shapes as shown on the first 6 shapes. Describe the pattern. Which shapes would most likely come next? Place those shapes as shown. Trace the shapes. Use shapes to copy the pattern. Point to each shape as you describe the pattern. Draw and color the shape pattern.

Share and Show

1

2

3

DIRECTIONS 1–3. Use shapes to copy the pattern. Which part of the pattern repeats over and over again? Circle that part. Which two shapes most likely come next? Draw and color the shapes.

Name ______________________________

4

5

6

DIRECTIONS 4–6. Use shapes to copy the pattern. Circle the part of the pattern that repeats over and over. Which two shapes most likely come next? Draw and color the shapes.

Problem Solving • Applications Real World

WRITE Math

7

_______ _______ _______ _______

8

DIRECTIONS 7. The shape pattern is square, circle. Draw to extend the pattern. **8.** Draw to show what you know about extending a shape pattern.

HOME ACTIVITY • Have your child use household objects to make a simple repeating shape pattern. Have him or her tell what would most likely come next in the pattern.

Name ____________________

Algebra: Extend a Shape Pattern

Learning Objective You will extend a shape pattern.

1

2

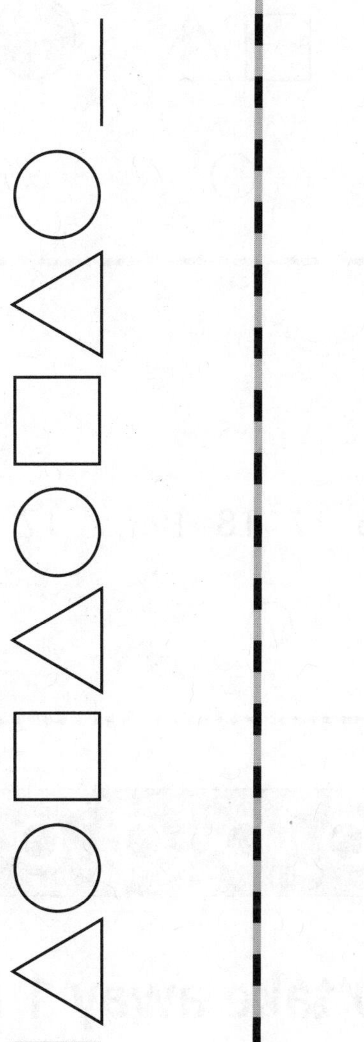

3

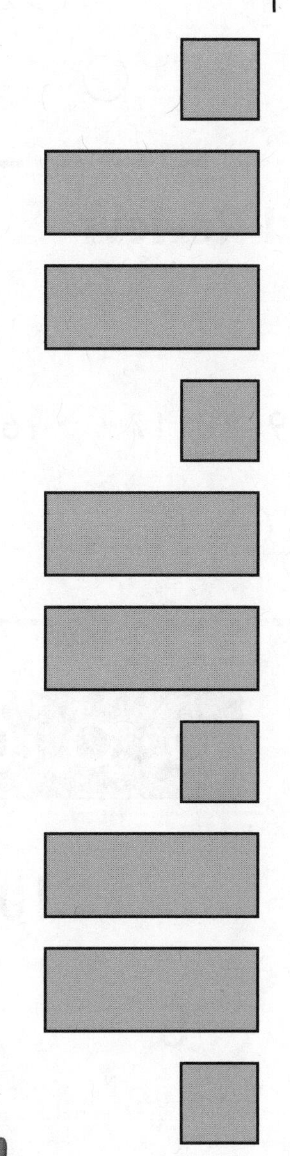

DIRECTIONS 1–3. Use shapes to copy the pattern. Which two shapes most likely come next? Draw and color the shapes.

Lesson Check

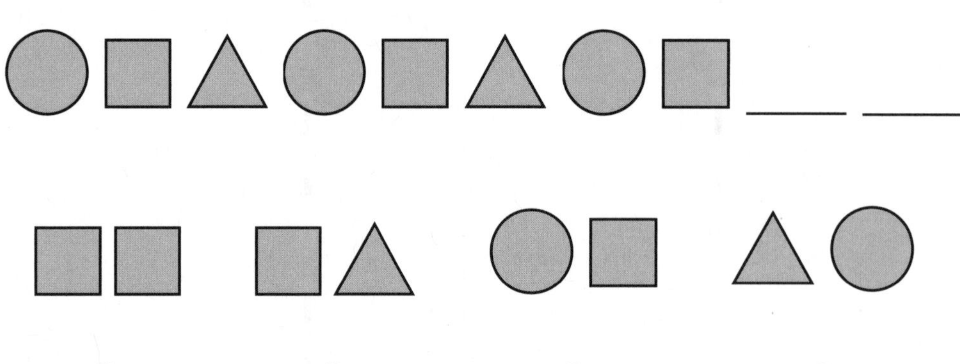

Spiral Review

16 19 18 17 16 17 18 19 17 16 18 19 19 16 17 18

10 take away 1 is ___

5 9 10 11

DIRECTIONS 1. Which shapes would most likely come next in the shape pattern? Mark under your answer. 2. Which shows the numbers in counting order? Mark under your answer. 3. How many are left? Circle your answer.

Name ______________________________

Find a Pattern • Number Patterns

Essential Question How can you solve problems by using the strategy *find a pattern*?

Learning Objective You will use the strategy *find a pattern* to solve problems.

Unlock the Problem

DIRECTIONS Read to describe the pattern. Trace the numbers to copy the pattern. Which part of the pattern repeats again and again? Trace the circle around that part.

Try Another Problem

1

2 ✓

1 1 2 1 1 2 1 1 2

3 ✓

1 2 2 1 2 2 1 2 2

DIRECTIONS Read to describe the pattern. **1.** Trace the numbers to copy the pattern. Which part of the pattern repeats again and again? Trace that part. **2–3.** Write the numbers to copy the pattern. Which part of the pattern repeats again and again? Circle that part.

Name ______________________

Share and Show

4 2 2 3 2 2 2 3 2 2 2 3

5 1 2 3 1 2 3 1 2 3

6 1 2 1 1 2 1 1 2 1

DIRECTIONS 4–6. Read to describe the pattern. Write the numbers to copy the pattern. Which part of the pattern repeats again and again? Circle that part.

On Your Own

7

WRITE Math

1 2 1 ___ 1 2

8

DIRECTIONS 7. Which number is missing in this pattern? Write the number where it belongs. **8.** Draw to show what you know about a number pattern.

HOME ACTIVITY • Have your child tell about the part of a number pattern that repeats again and again.

Name ______________________________

Problem Solving: Find a Pattern • Number Patterns

Learning Objective You will use the strategy *find a pattern* to solve problems.

1 1 2 3 1 2 3 1 2 3

2 1 2 1 1 2 1 1 2 1

3 2 2 1 2 2 1 2 2 1

DIRECTIONS 1–3. Read to describe the pattern. Write the numbers to copy the pattern. Which part of the pattern repeats again and again? Circle that part.

Lesson Check

2 1 2 2 1 2 2 1 2

1 1 1	2 1 2	2 2 2	1 2 3
○	○	○	○

Spiral Review

5 + 3 = ____

10	8	5	3
○	○	○	○

7 8 9 10

DIRECTIONS 1. Which set shows the part of the number pattern that repeats? Mark under your answer. **2.** Mark under your answer to show how many in all. **3.** How many umbrellas? Circle your answer.

Name ___________________________________

Algebra: Extend a Number Pattern

Essential Question How can you extend a number pattern?

Learning Objective You will extend a number pattern.

Listen and Draw

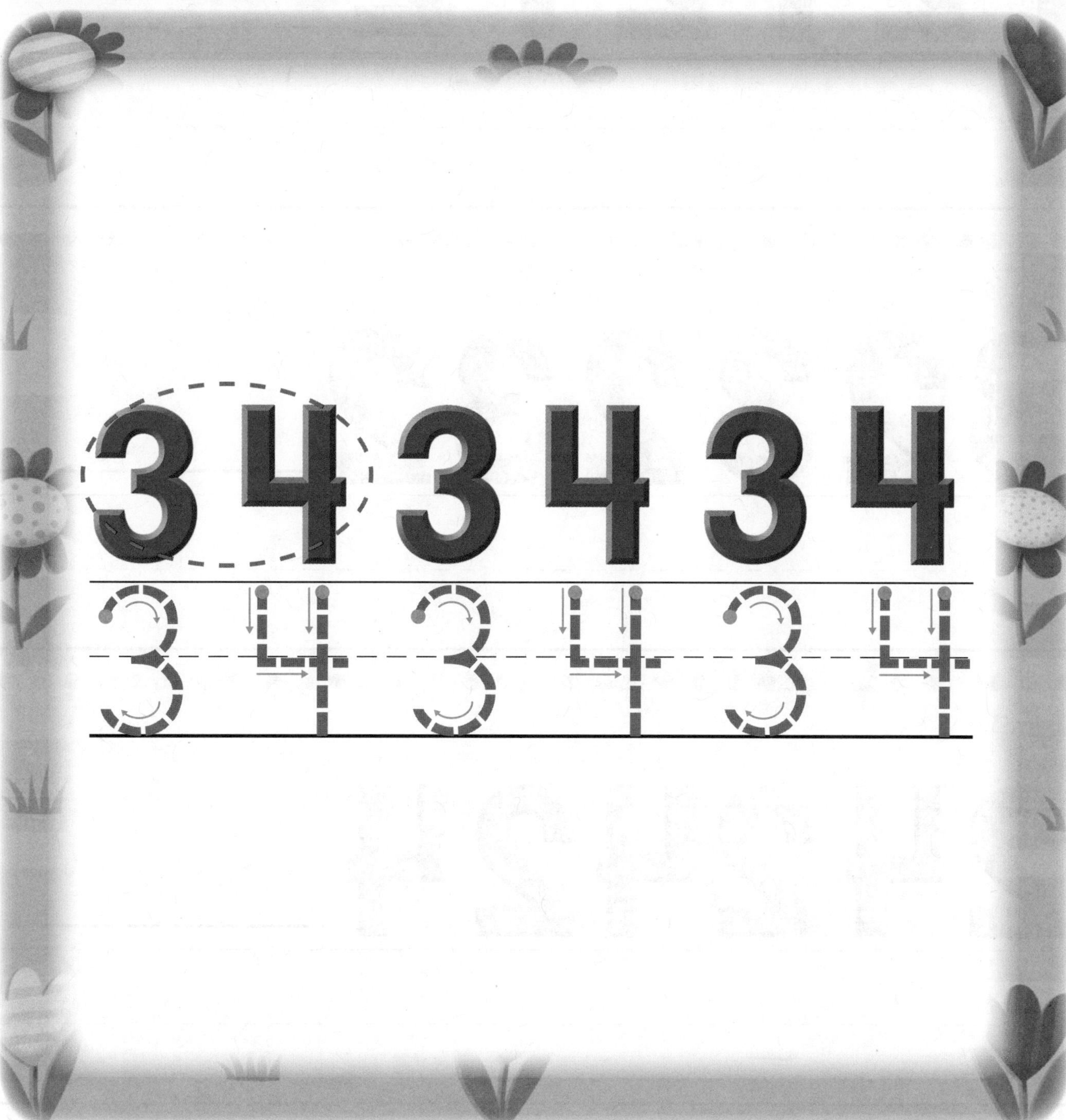

DIRECTIONS Read to describe the pattern. Trace the number pattern. Which part repeats again and again? Trace the circle around that part. Talk about which numbers are most likely to come next.

Share and Show

1

1 2 1 2 1 2 ___ ___

2

3 2 3 2 3 2 ___ ___

3

2 4 2 4 2 4 ___ ___

DIRECTIONS 1–3. Look at the pattern. Circle the part of the pattern that repeats over and over again. Which numbers are most likely to come next? Write the numbers to copy and extend the pattern.

Name ______________________________

1 1 2 1 1 2 1 1 2 ___ ___

5

3 2 2 3 2 2 3 2 2 ___ ___

6

3 4 5 3 4 5 3 4 5 ___ ___

DIRECTIONS 4–6. Look at the pattern. What part of the pattern repeats over and over again? Circle that part. Which numbers are most likely to come next? Write the numbers to copy and extend the pattern.

Problem Solving • Applications

WRITE Math

7

442

8

DIRECTIONS 7. The number pattern is 4, 4, 2. Write to extend the number pattern. 8. Draw to show what you know about extending a number pattern.

HOME ACTIVITY • Place 8 pieces of paper in a row. Write the numbers 1 and 2 to show a pattern of 1/2/1/2/1/2. Ask your child to write which numbers are most likely to come next.

Name ______________________________

Algebra: Extend a Number Pattern

Learning Objective You will extend a number pattern.

1

2 3 2 3 2 3 ___ ___

2

3 1 1 3 1 1 3 1 1 ___ ___

3

3 4 3 4 3 4 ___ ___

DIRECTIONS 1–3. Look at the pattern. Circle the part that repeats over and over again. Which numbers are most likely to come next? Write the numbers to copy and extend the pattern.

Lesson Check

1 322322322

1 2 ○ 2 2 ○ 3 2 ○ 3 4 ○

Spiral Review

  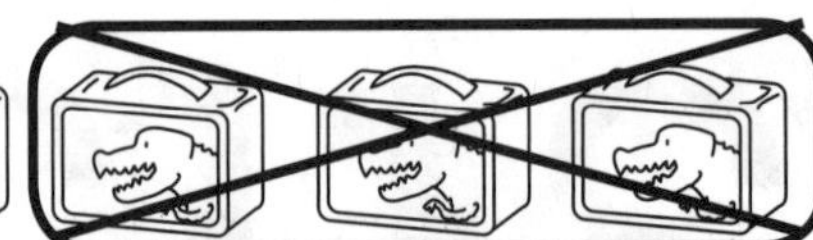

5 – 3 = ___

2 3 4 5

1 ○ 2 ○ 3 ○ 4 ○

DIRECTIONS 1. Which numbers are most likely to come next in the number pattern? Mark under your answer. **2.** How many lunch boxes are left? Circle your answer. **3.** How many sides does the square have? Mark under your answer.

Name ______________________________

Algebra: Describe and Copy a Growing Pattern

Essential Question How can you describe and copy a growing pattern?

Learning Objective You will describe and copy a growing pattern.

Listen and Draw

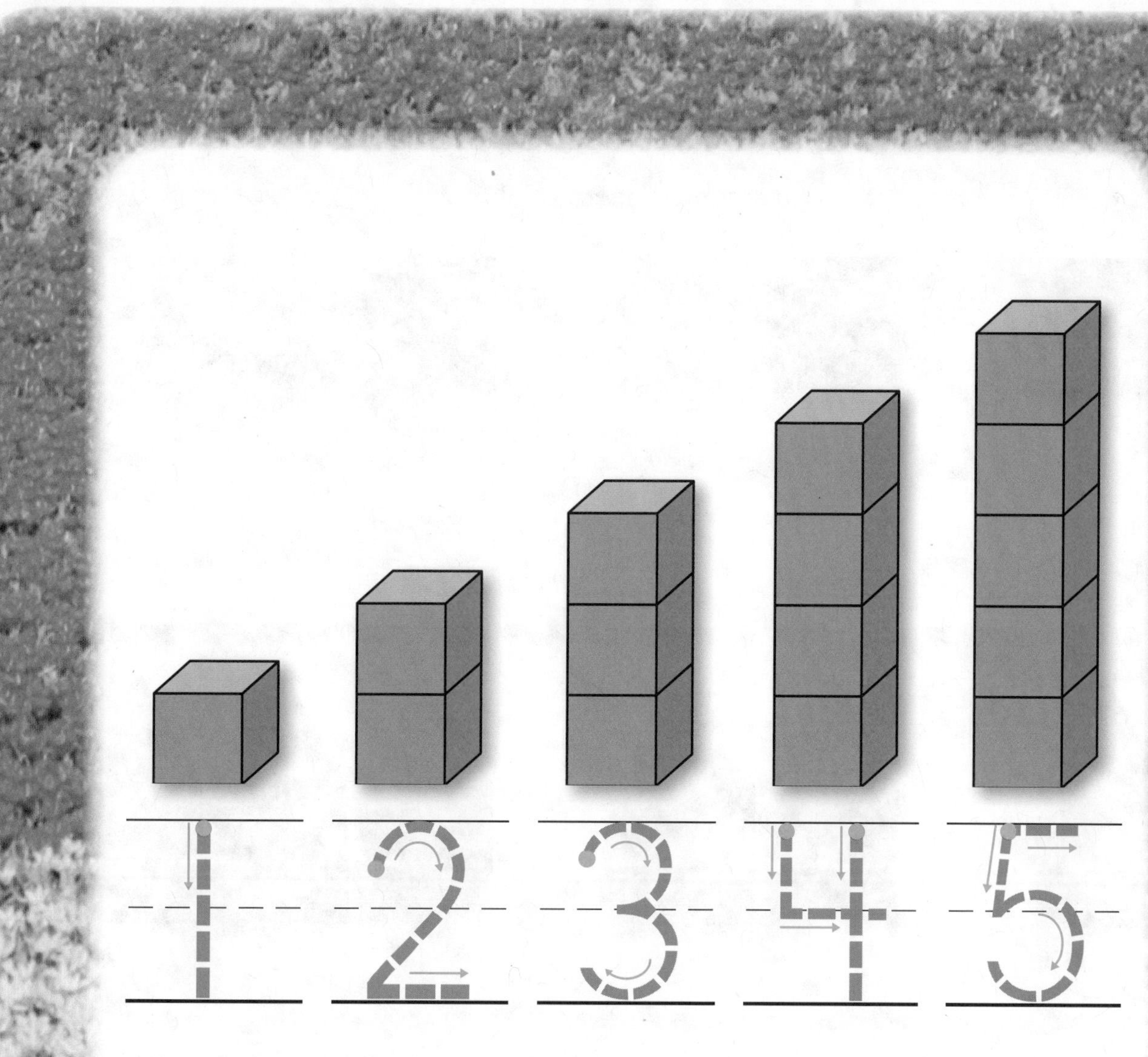

DIRECTIONS Point to the block towers, starting with the block on the left. Trace how many blocks in each tower. Tell how the towers change each time.

Share and Show

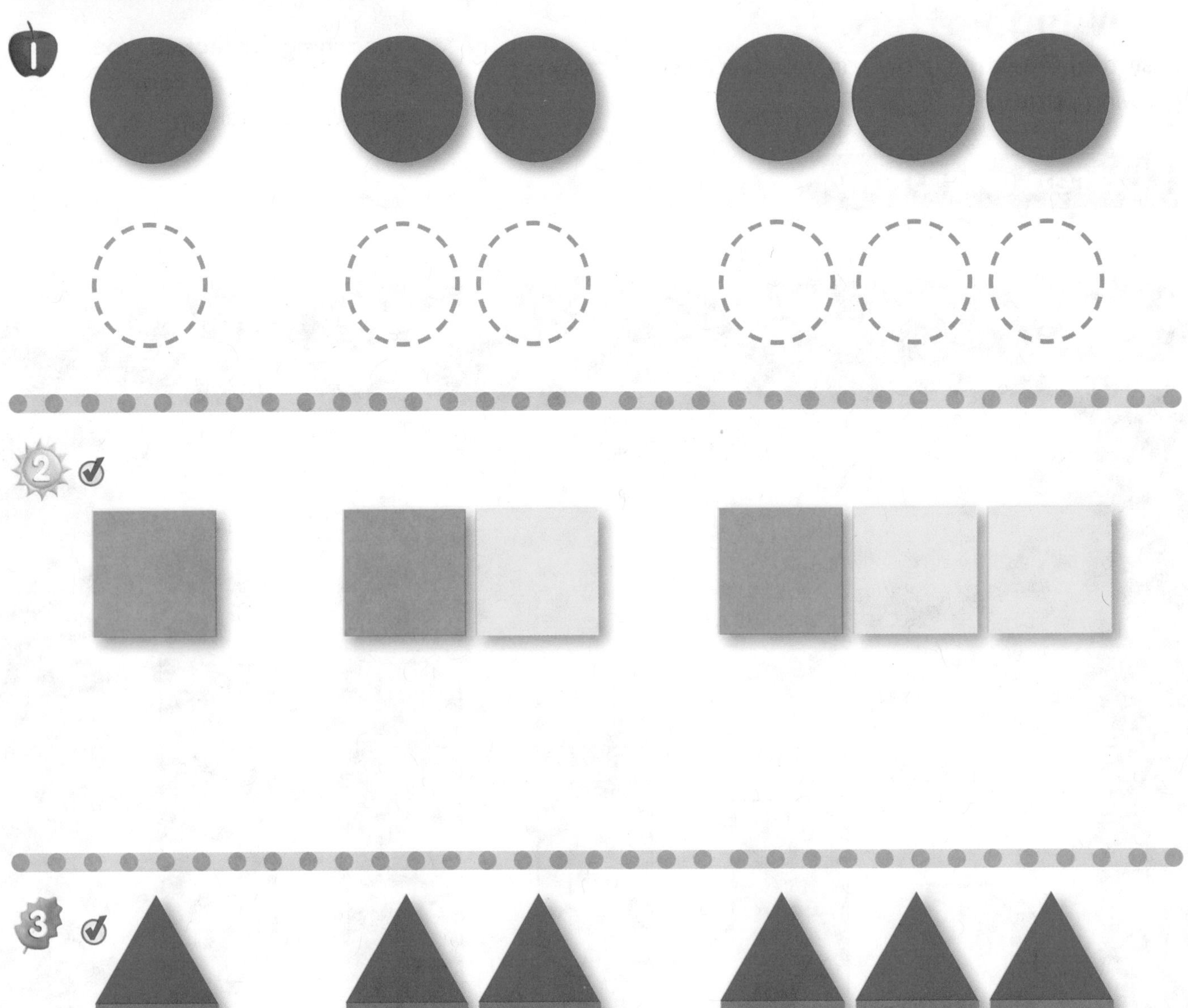

DIRECTIONS Read to describe the pattern. Place shapes to copy the pattern. **1.** Trace and color the pattern. **2–3.** Draw and color the pattern.

Name ______________________

4

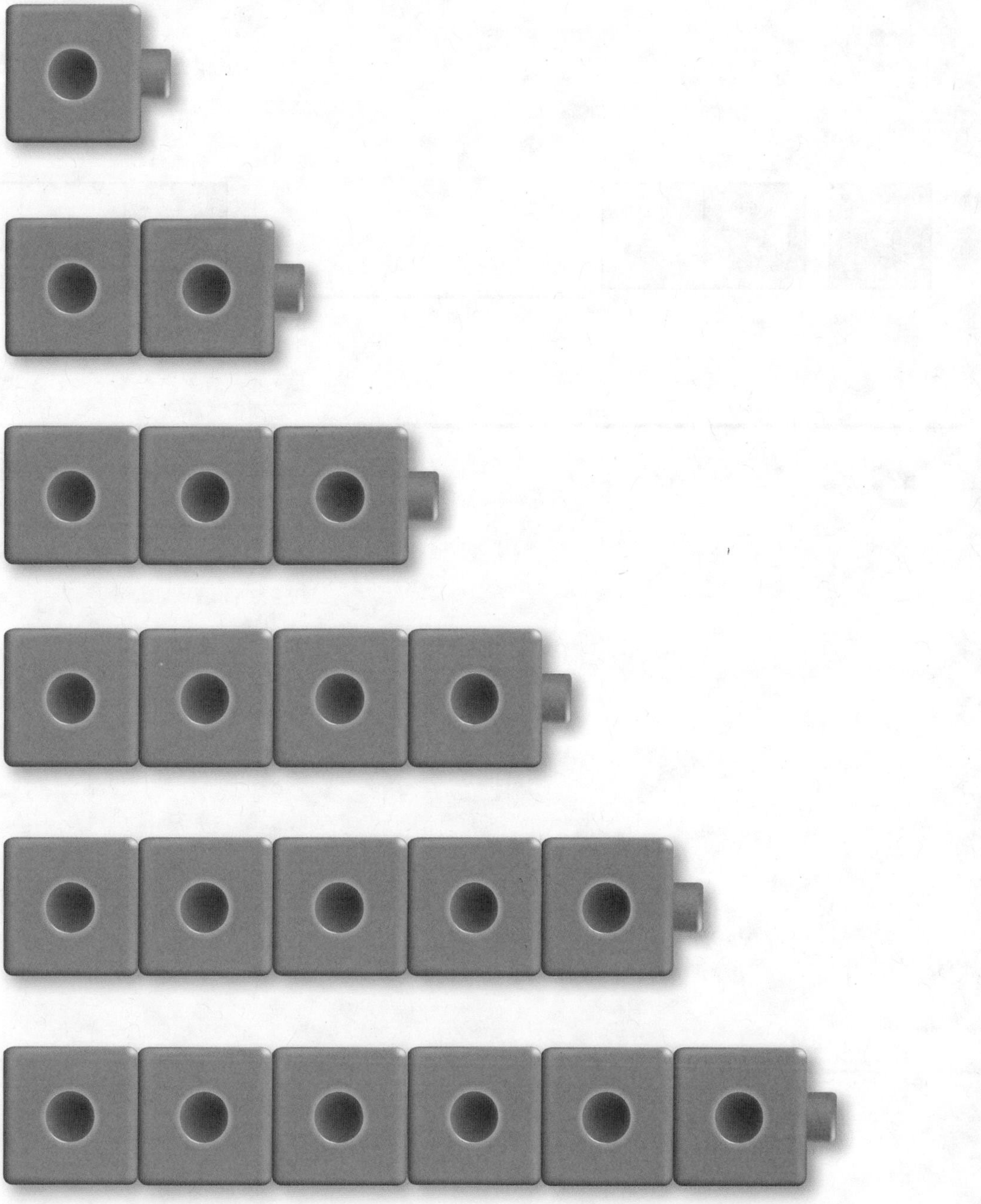

DIRECTIONS 4. Write how many cubes in each train. Read to describe the growing pattern.

Problem Solving • Applications Real World

WRITE Math

5

______

6

DIRECTIONS 5. What is missing in this growing pattern? Draw and color to show what is missing. 6. Draw and color to show what you know about a growing pattern.

HOME ACTIVITY • Have your child show you a growing pattern using household objects.

Name ______________________________

Algebra: Describe and Copy a Growing Pattern

Learning Objective You will describe and copy a growing pattern.

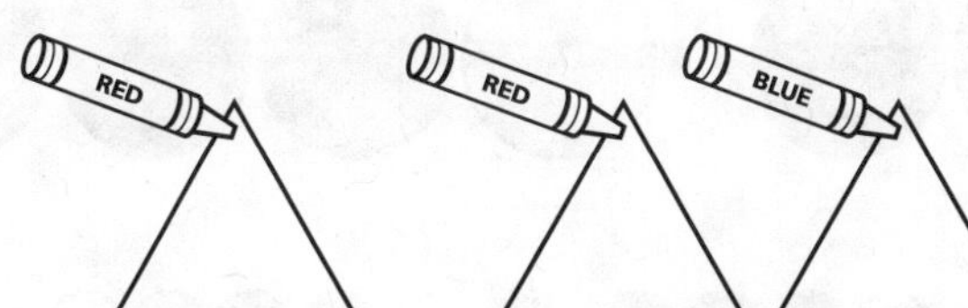

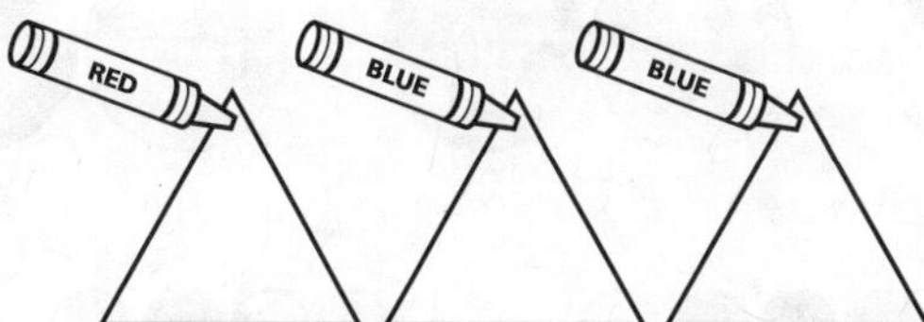

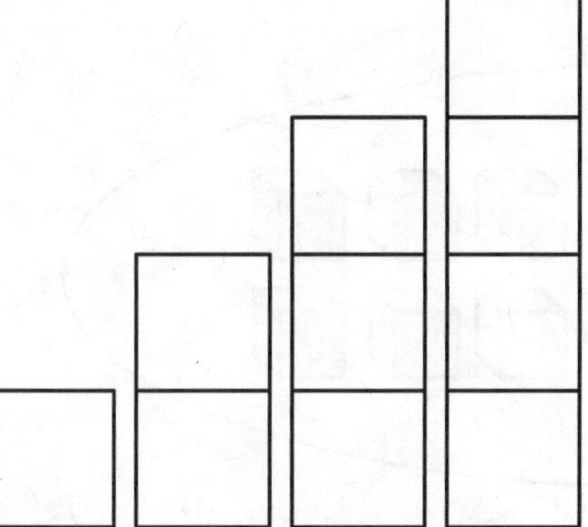

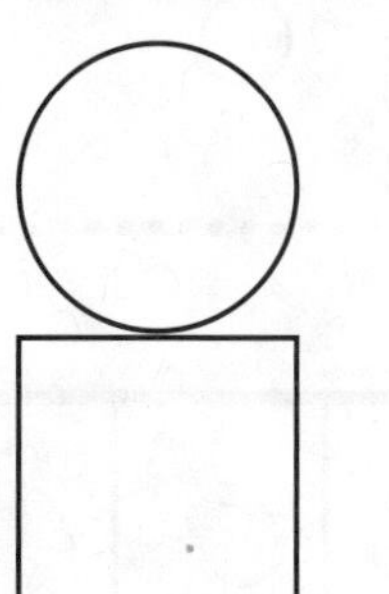

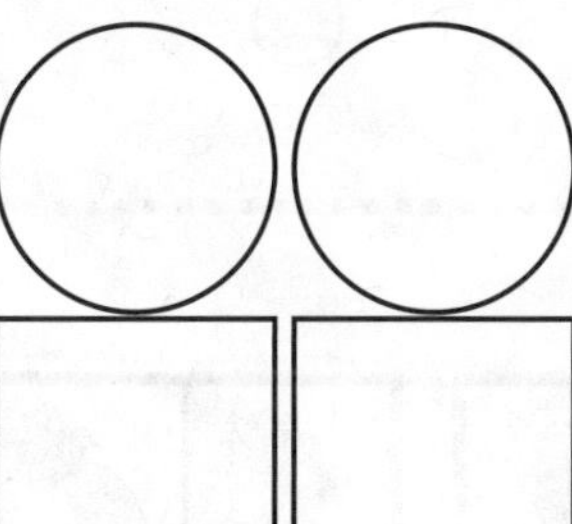

DIRECTIONS 1–3. Read to describe the pattern. Place shapes to copy the pattern. Draw and color the pattern.

Lesson Check

1

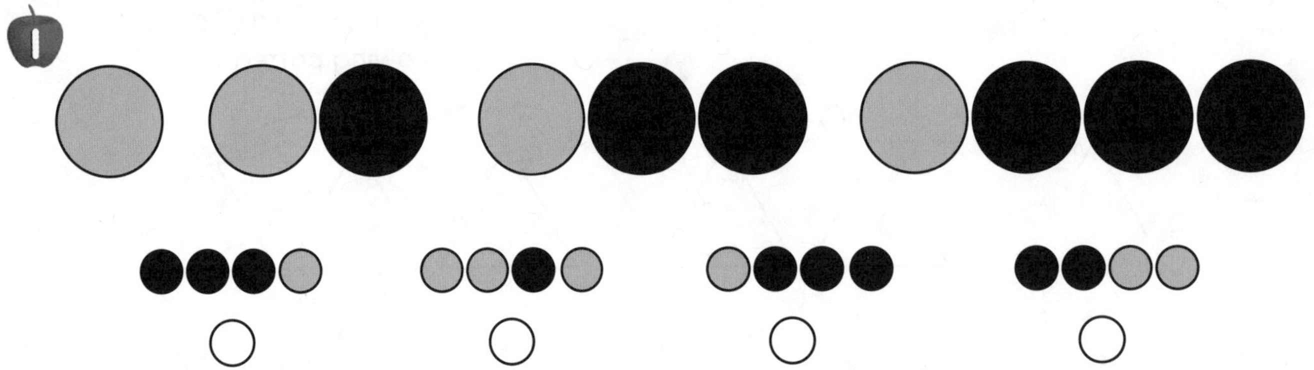

Spiral Review

2

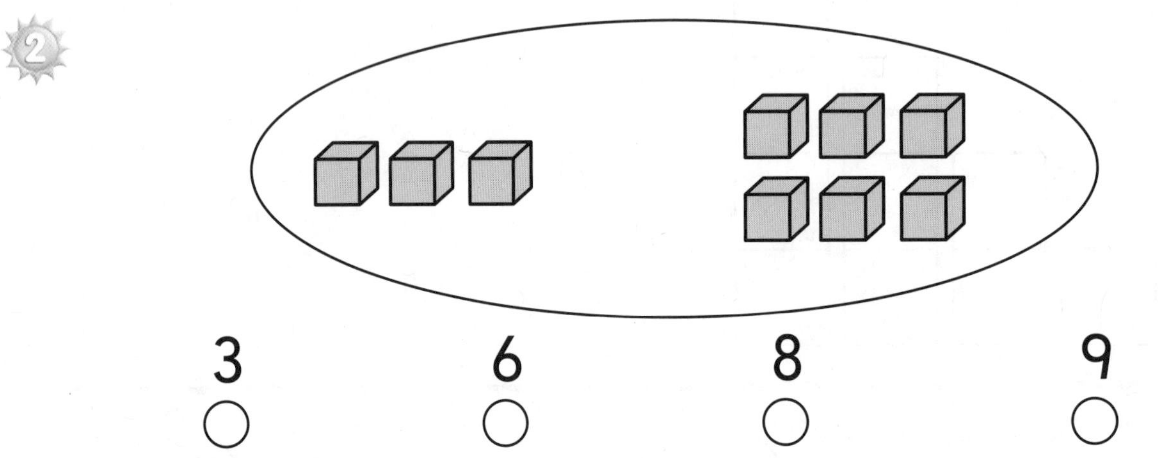

3 6 8 9

3

17 18 19 20

DIRECTIONS 1. Which pattern matches the growing pattern? Mark under your answer. **2.** How many blocks in all? Mark under your answer. **3.** How many pineapples? Circle your answer.

Name ____________________

Algebra: Extend a Growing Pattern

Essential Question How can you extend a growing pattern?

Learning Objective You will extend a growing pattern.

Listen and Draw Real World

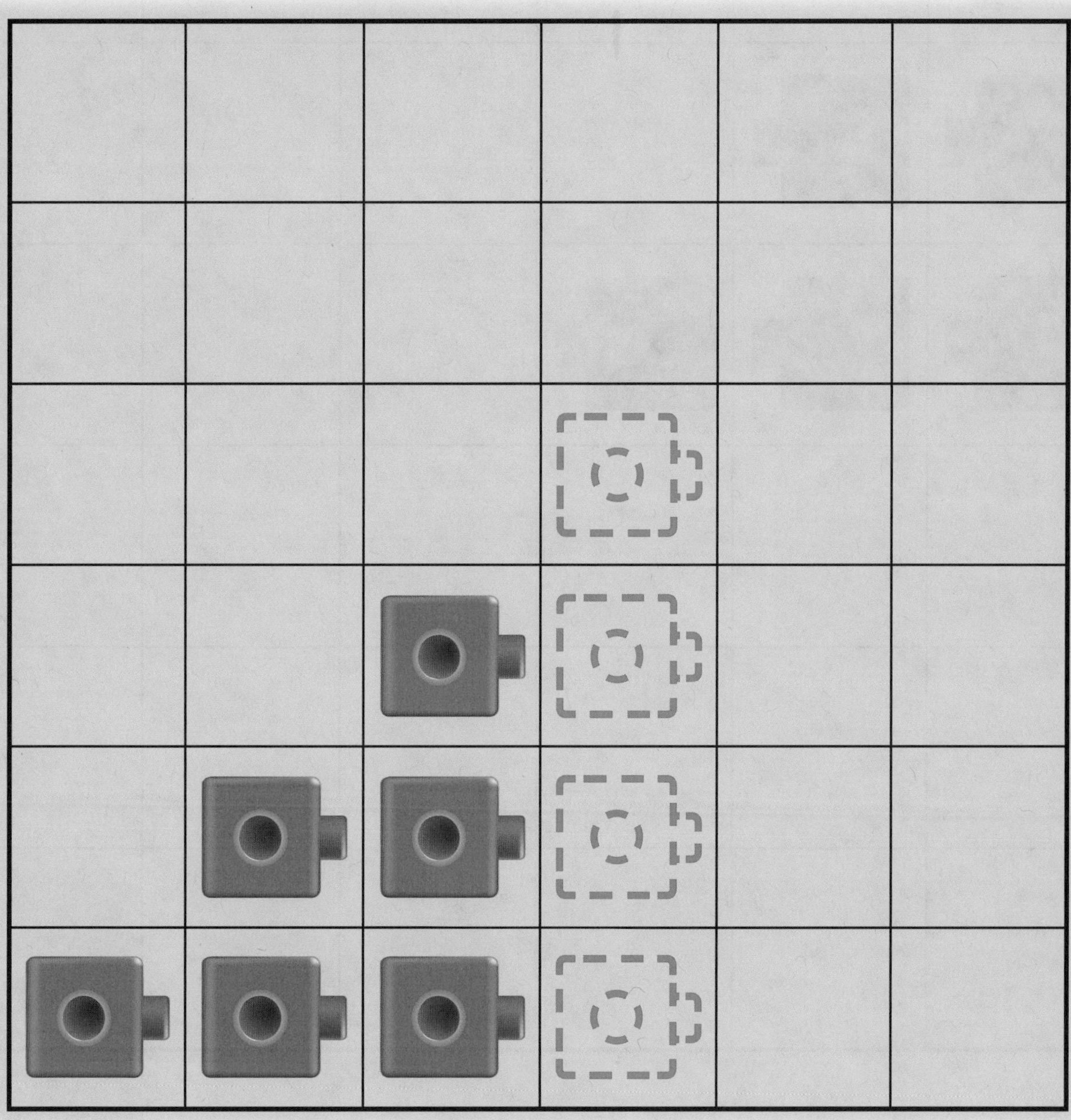

DIRECTIONS Look at the growing pattern. Tell about the pattern. Use connecting cubes to extend the pattern. Draw and color the cubes.

Share and Show

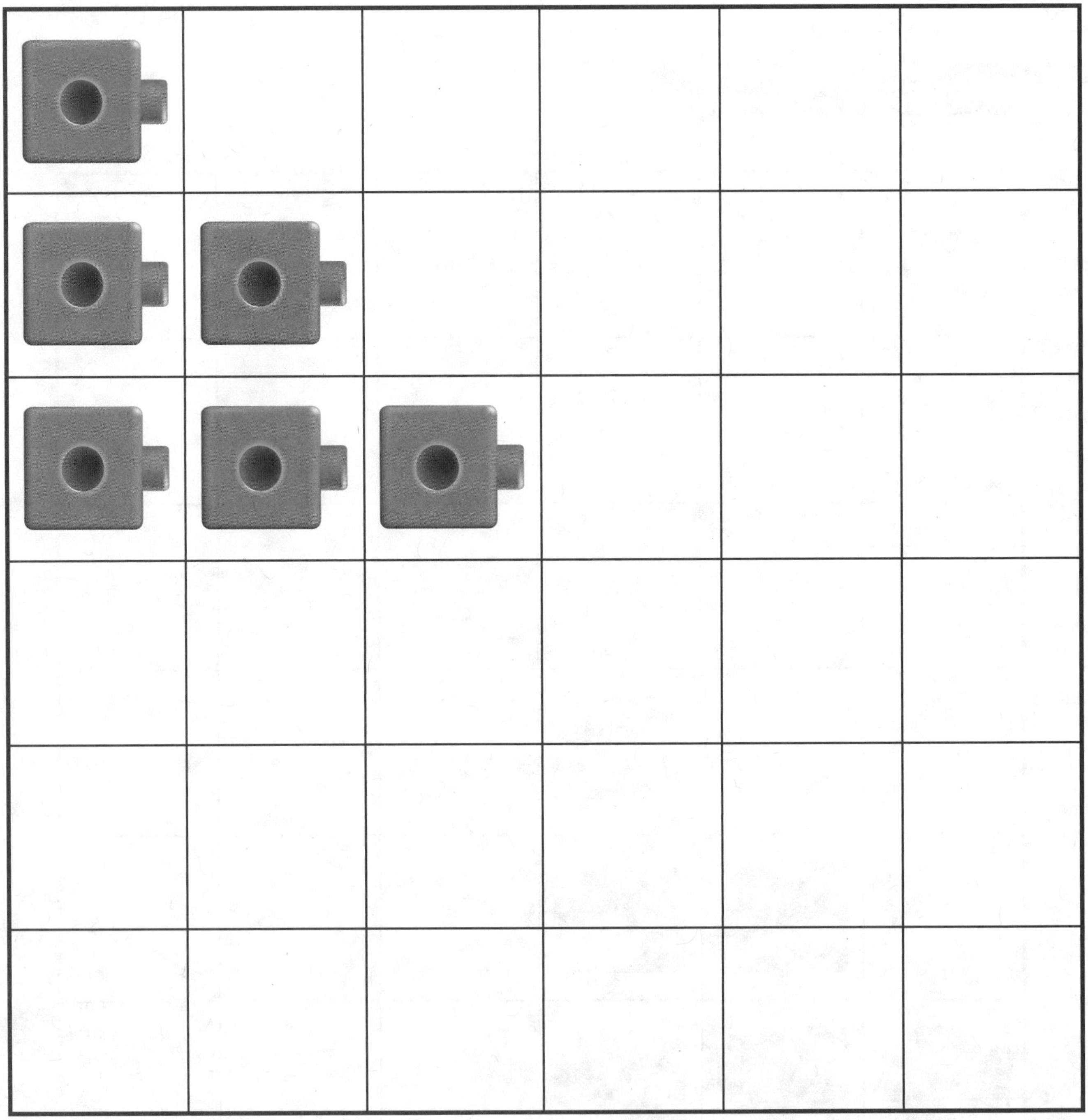

DIRECTIONS 1. Look at the growing pattern. Tell about the pattern. Use connecting cubes to extend the pattern. Draw and color the cubes.

Name ______________________________

2

3

4

DIRECTIONS Look at the growing pattern. 2. Draw squares in any color to extend the pattern two times. 3. Draw flowers to extend the pattern in the rest of the flower pots. 4. Draw dots to extend the pattern one time.

Problem Solving • Applications Real World

WRITE Math

5

DIRECTIONS 5. Michael used connecting cubes to make a growing pattern. He shows his 3 shapes to Madison. Madison correctly puts connecting cubes in the grid to show what comes next in the pattern. Draw what she did.

HOME ACTIVITY • Show your child a growing pattern using toothpicks. First build a triangle using one toothpick for each side. Then build a triangle using two toothpicks on each side. Next build a triangle using three toothpicks on each side. Have your child build the next triangle in the growing pattern.

Name ___________________________________

Algebra: Extend a Growing Pattern

Learning Objective You will extend a growing pattern.

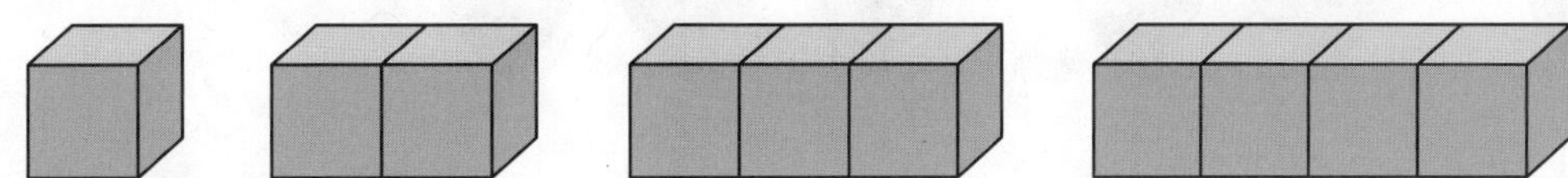

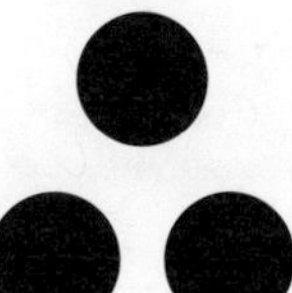

DIRECTIONS Look at the growing pattern. **1.** Draw to extend the pattern one time. **2.** Draw butterflies to extend the pattern two times. **3.** Draw rays on the suns to extend the pattern two times. **4.** Draw dots to extend the pattern one time.

Lesson Check

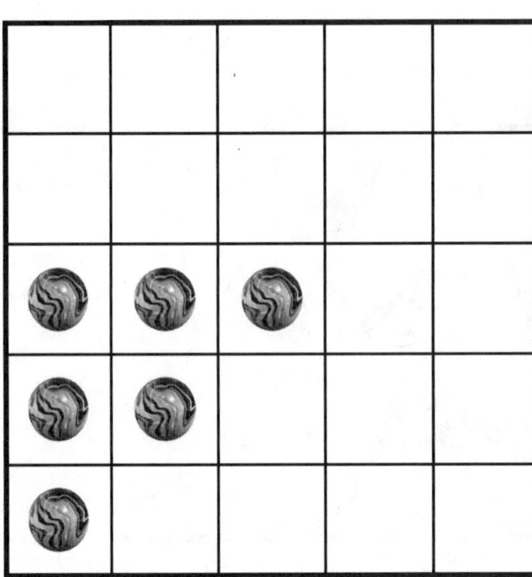

Spiral Review

15

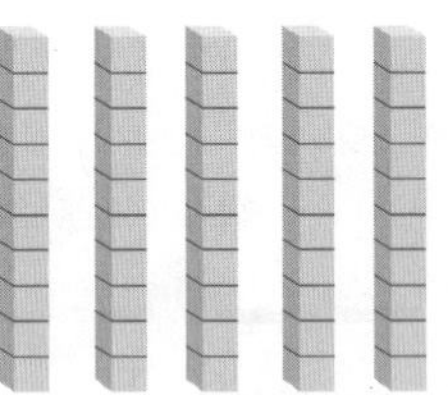

5 15 50

DIRECTIONS 1. Look at the growing pattern. Extend the pattern one time. 2. Look at the growing pattern. Extend the pattern two times. 3. Look at the number. Write the number that is one less. Write the number that is one more. 4. Count by tens. Circle how many.

Name ______________________________

Algebra: Create a Pattern

Essential Question How can you create a pattern?

Learning Objective You will create a pattern.

Listen and Draw

DIRECTIONS Place a handful of cubes in the workspace. Move the cubes to the pattern strip to create a pattern. Draw and color the pattern. Describe the pattern. Talk about the part that repeats again and again.

Share and Show

1

2

DIRECTIONS 1. Use counters to make a pattern. Draw and color your pattern. Circle the part that repeats again and again. **2.** Use pattern blocks to make a pattern. Draw and color your pattern. Circle the part that repeats again and again.

Name ______________________________

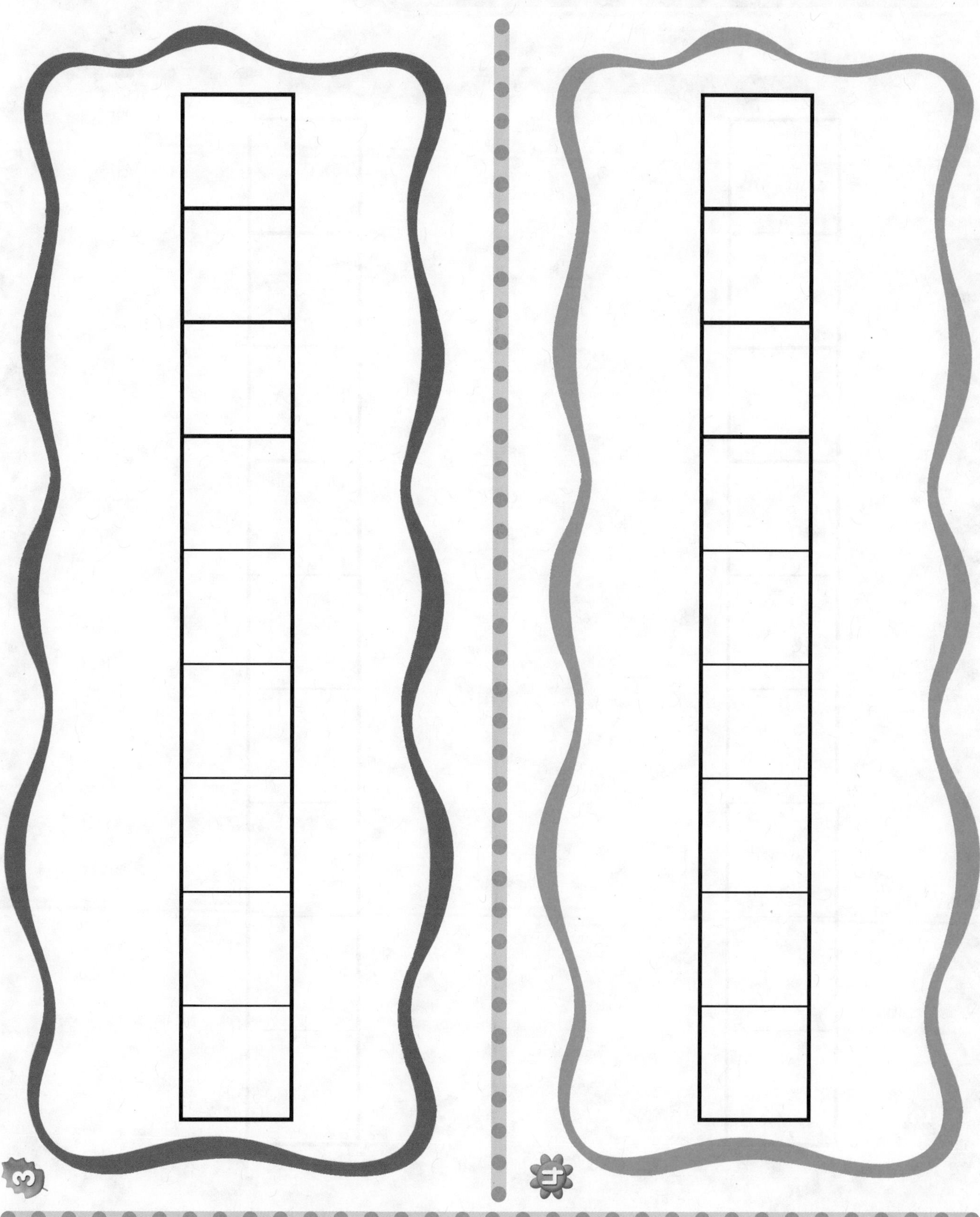

DIRECTIONS 3–4. Use shapes to create a pattern. Draw and color your pattern. Circle the part that repeats again and again. Describe your pattern to a friend.

Problem Solving • Applications Real World

WRITE Math

5

6

DIRECTIONS 5. Use objects to create a pattern. Draw and color the pattern.
6. Draw to show what you know about creating a pattern.

Home Activity • Have your child use household objects such as macaroni, buttons, or coins to create a pattern. Have him or her describe the pattern.

Name ___

Hands On • Algebra: Create a Pattern

Learning Objective You will create a pattern.

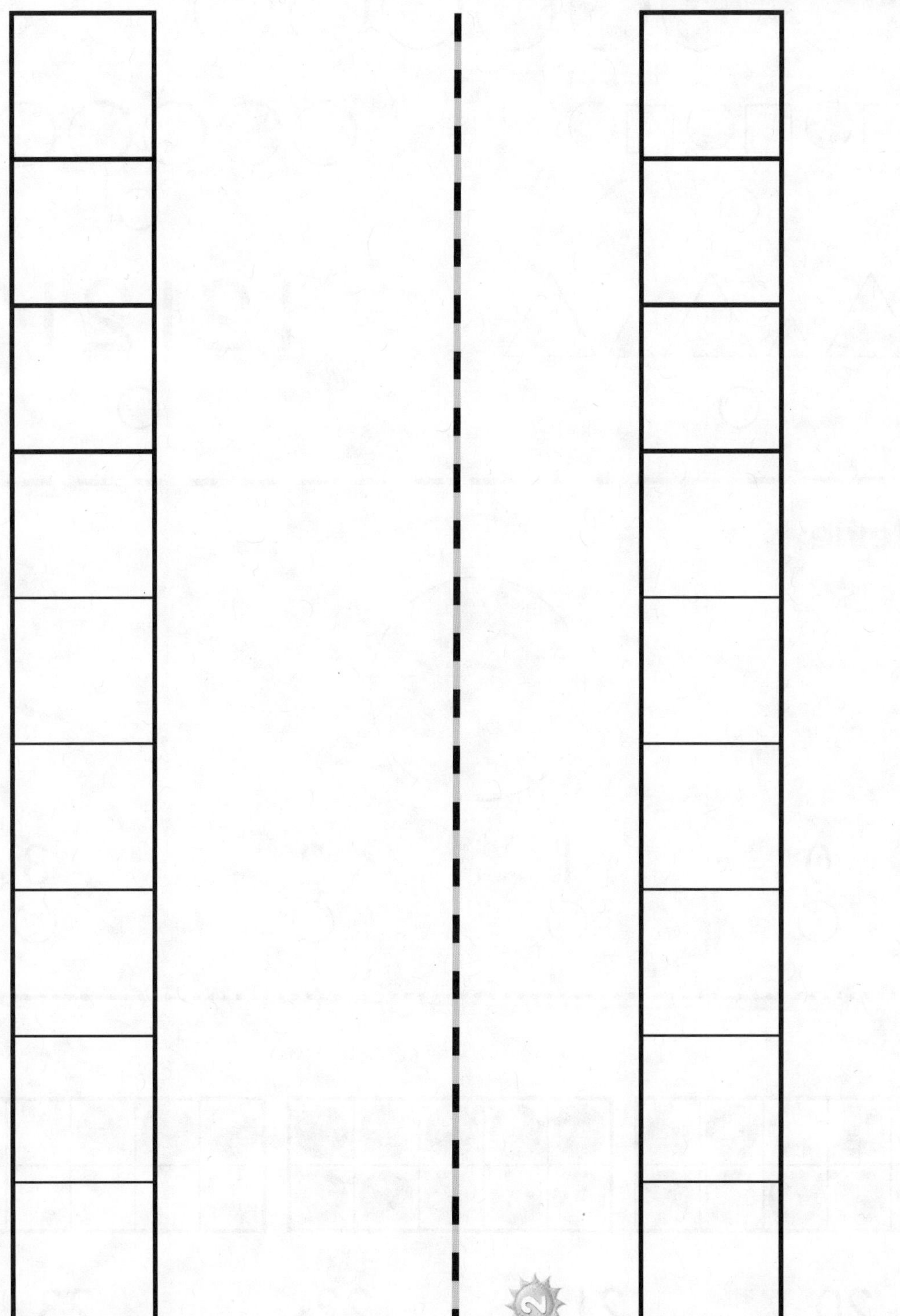

DIRECTIONS 1. Use counters to make a pattern. Draw and color your pattern. Circle the part that repeats again and again. 2. Use pattern blocks to make a pattern. Draw and color your pattern. Circle the part that repeats again and again.

Lesson Check

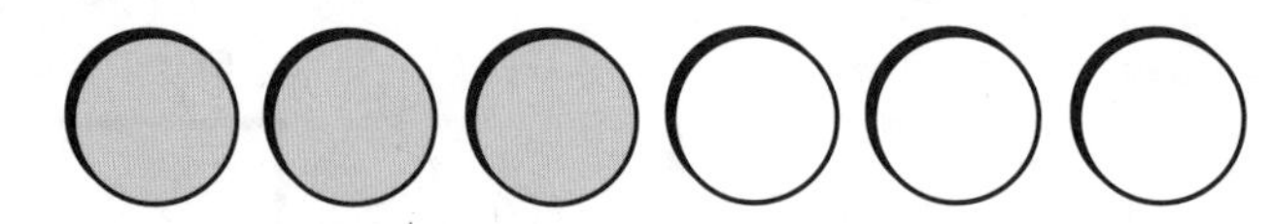

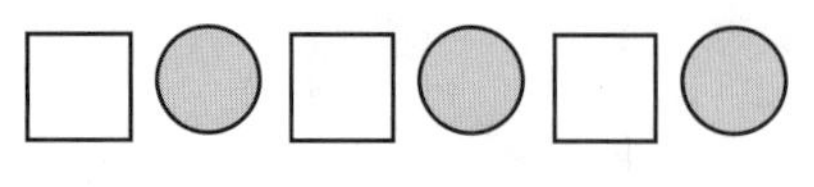

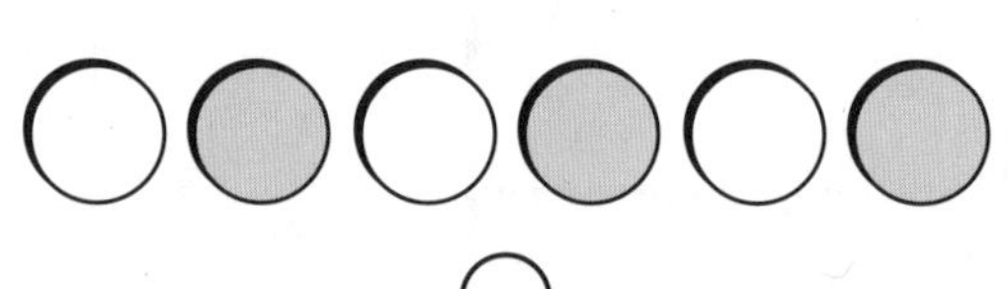

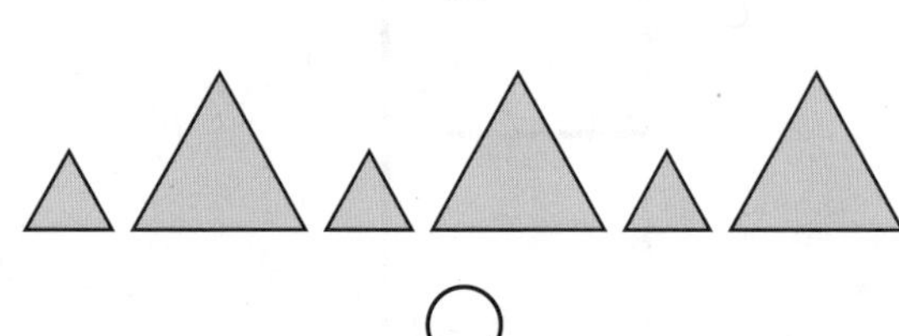

121212

Spiral Review

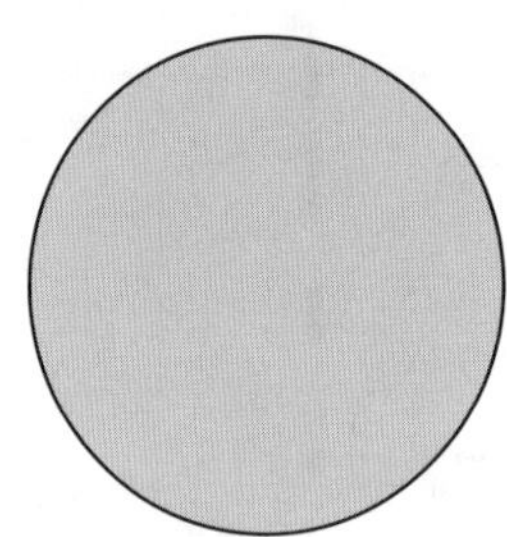

0 1 2 3

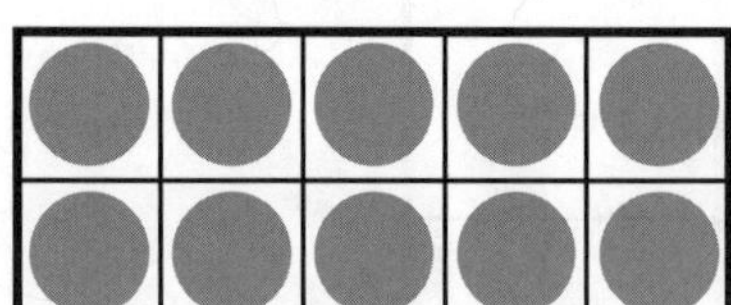

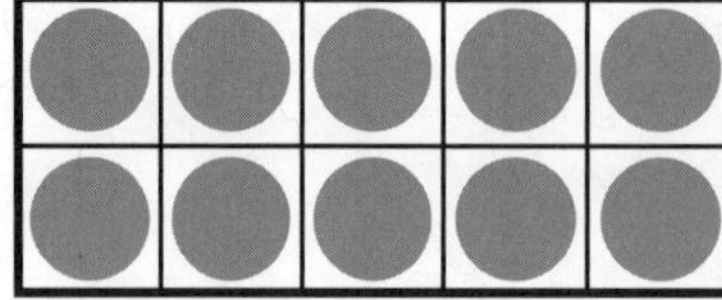

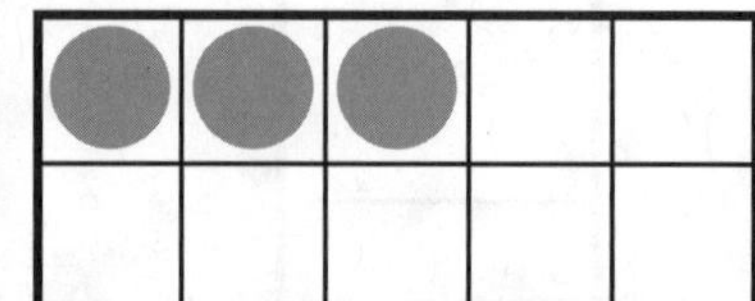

20 21 22 23

DIRECTIONS 1. Which pattern could you create from these counters? Mark under your answer. **2.** How many straight sides does the circle have? Mark under your answer. **3.** How many counters? Circle your answer.

Name ____________________

Our Senses
Develop Concepts

Use with *ScienceFusion* pages 1–4.

1

2

3

4
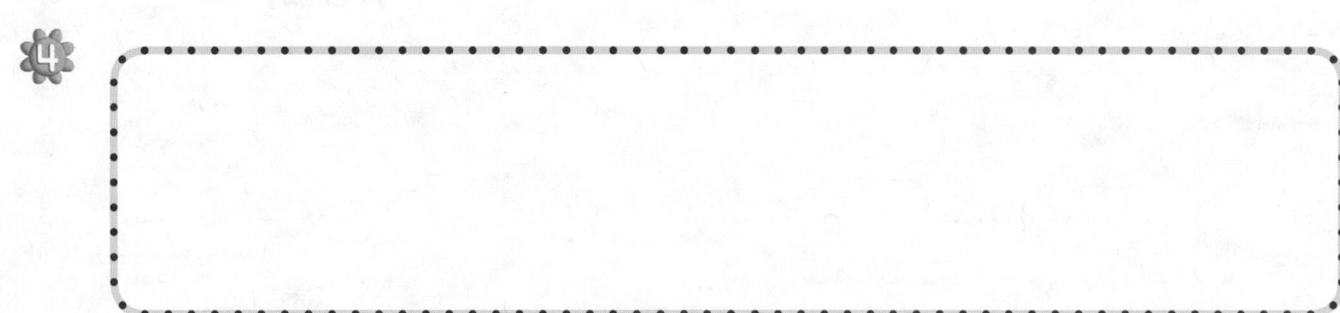

DIRECTIONS 1. Draw one object you can hear. 2. Draw two objects you can smell. 3. Draw three objects you can see. 4. Draw four objects you can taste.

Sum It Up!

see

smell

taste

touch

hear

DIRECTIONS Draw to show what you know about your senses using popcorn.

Name ______________________________________

Recycling Paper
Develop Concepts

Use with *ScienceFusion* pages 103–104.

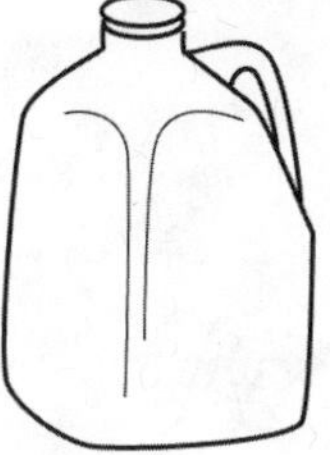

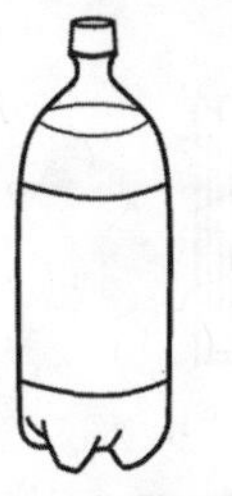
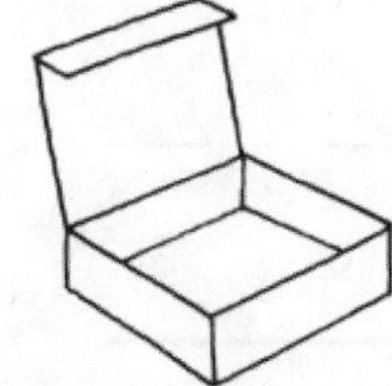

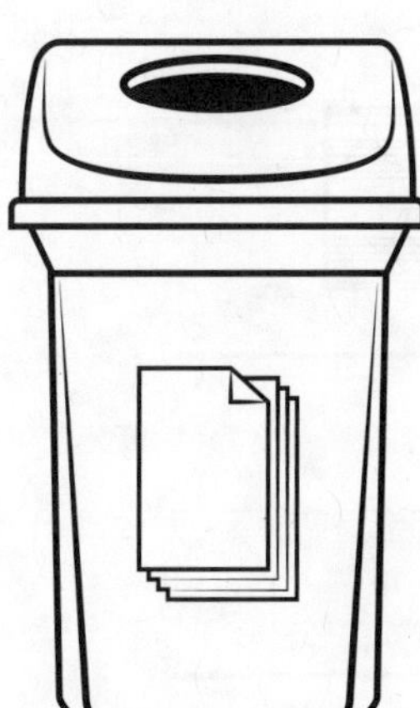

DIRECTIONS Draw a line from the object to its container.

Sum It Up!

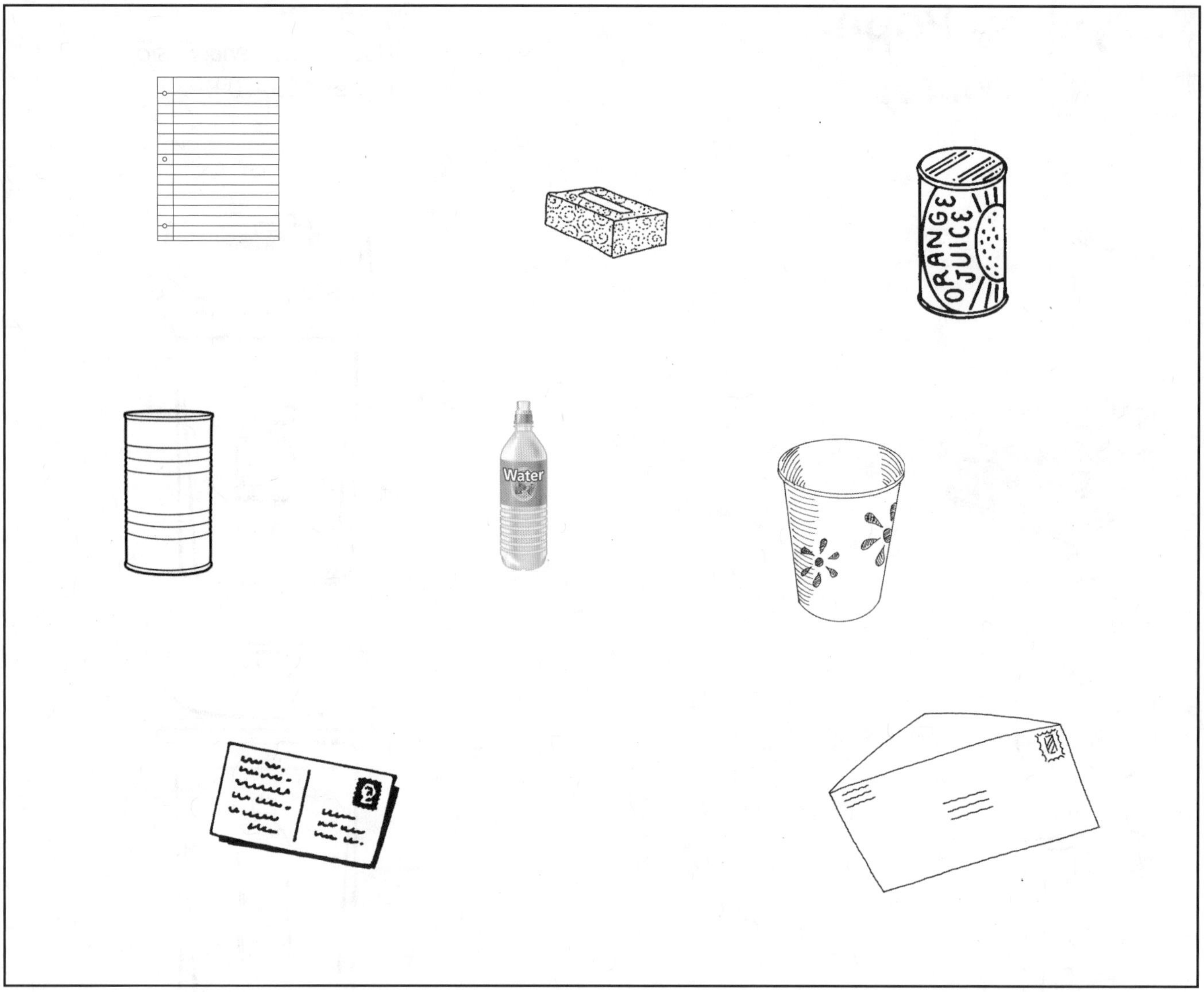

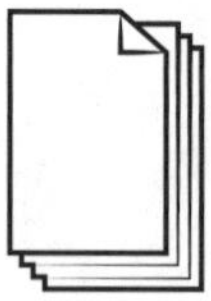

DIRECTIONS Count the metal cans, the objects made of paper, and the plastic bottles. Write how many of each object. Circle the number that is the greatest.

Name ______________________________

Rocks

Develop Concepts

Use with *ScienceFusion* pages 63–66.

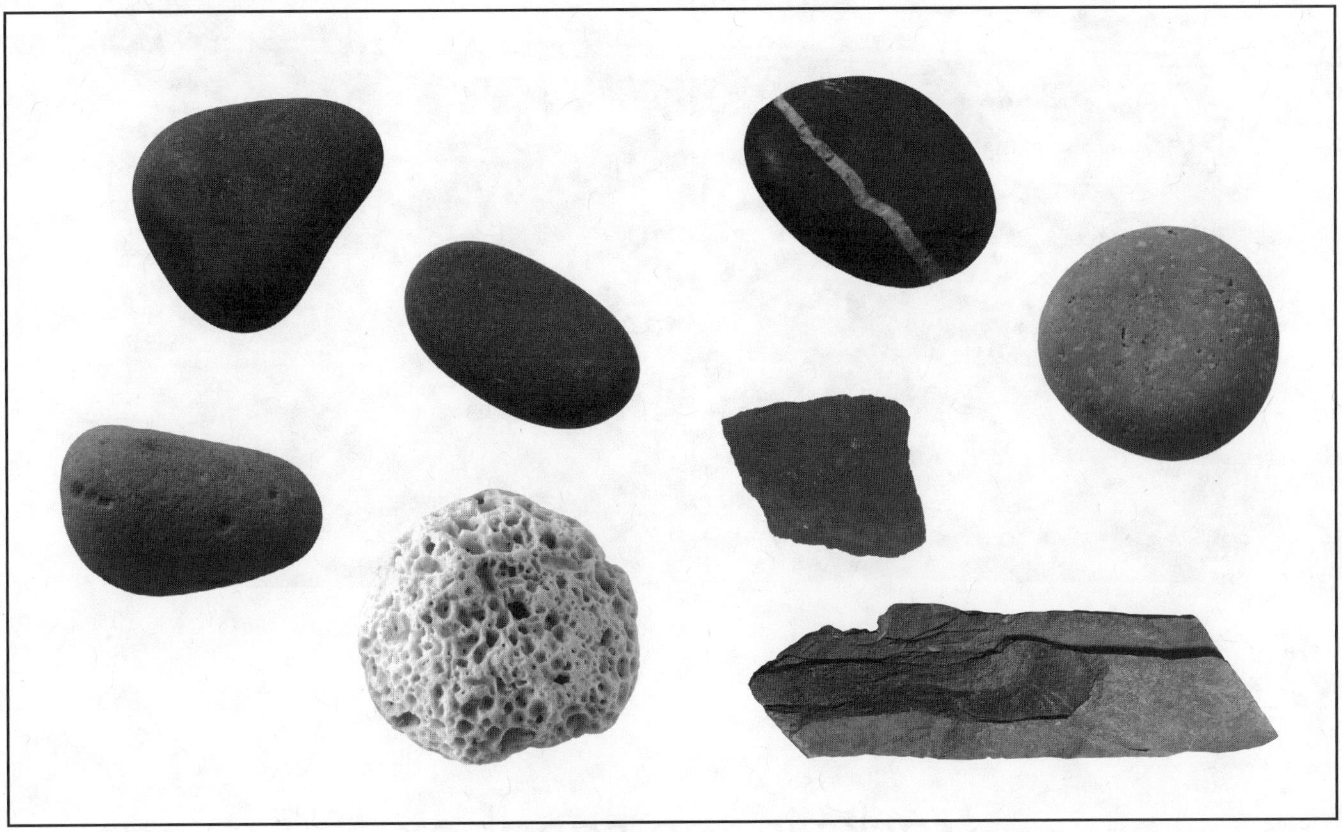

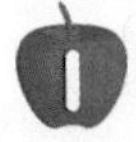

1 ____________

____________ rocks

2 ____________

I found ____________ rocks.

DIRECTIONS 1. These rocks have different sizes, shapes, and textures. Count the rocks. Write how many. **2.** Find some rocks. Write how many rocks you found.

Sum It Up!

3 ________

_ _ _ _ _ _ _ _

________ rocks in the sandbox

4 ________

_ _ _ _ _ _ _ _

________ rocks outside the sandbox

5 ________

_ _ _ _ _ _ _ _

________ rocks in all

DIRECTIONS 3. Count the rocks in the sandbox. Write how many. 4. Count the rocks outside the sandbox. Write how many. 5. Count all the rocks in the picture. Write how many.

Name ____________________

Living and Nonliving
Develop Concepts

Use with *ScienceFusion* pages 105–108.

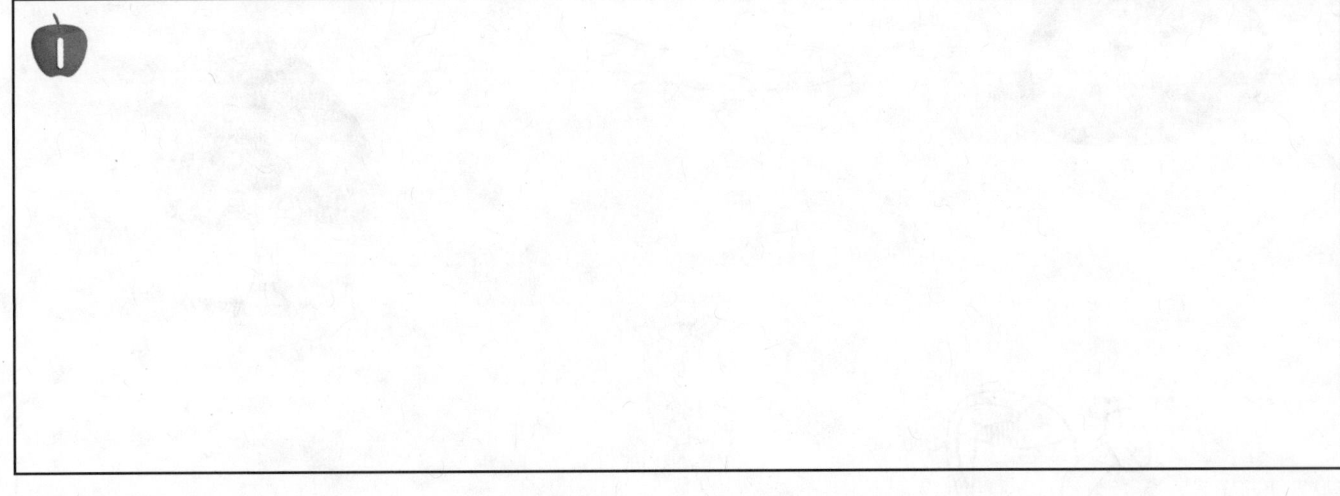

DIRECTIONS 1. Draw a picture of a living thing. 2. Draw a picture of a nonliving thing. 3. Draw a picture of a basic need of a living thing.

Sum It Up!

____

_ _ _ _ _ _ _ _ living things

____

____

_ _ _ _ _ _ _ _ nonliving things

____

DIRECTIONS Circle each living thing. Mark an X on each nonliving thing. Write how many living things. Write how many nonliving things.

Name ______________________________

Aquarium Design

Design It: Model Terrarium

Use with *ScienceFusion* pages 137–138.

5 + 3 = 8

DIRECTIONS Use two colors to color objects in the terrarium that models the addition sentence.

Develop Concepts

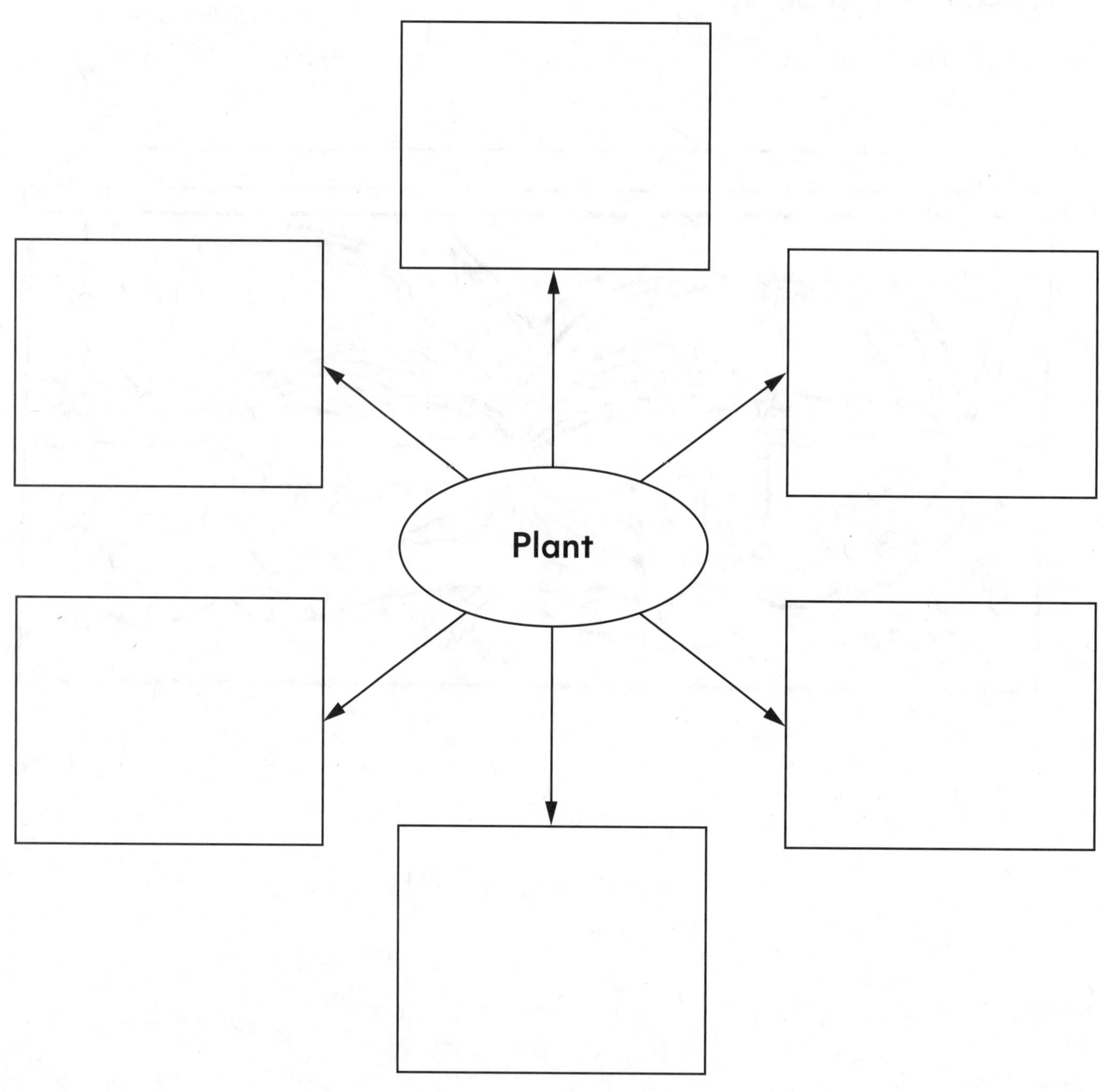

DIRECTIONS Describe the basic needs of a terrarium.

Name ________________________________

Many Animals

Develop Concepts

Use with *ScienceFusion* pages 109–112.

Animals with Different Coverings

feathers		______

scales	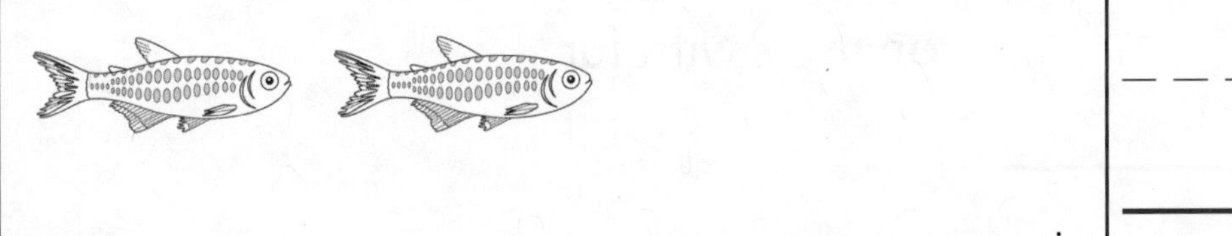	______

fur		______

DIRECTIONS 1–3. Count how many. Write the number.

Sum It Up!

4

animals with fur

5

animals with feathers

6

$6 - 3 =$

DIRECTIONS 4. Count the animals with fur. Write the number. 5. Count the animals with feathers. Write the number. 6. Complete the subtraction sentence that shows the difference between the two numbers.

Name ______________________________

Plants Grow and Change

Develop Concepts

Use with *ScienceFusion* pages 133–136.

DIRECTIONS 1. Draw to show what this seedling might grow into.

Sum It Up!

DIRECTIONS **2.** Count the seedlings. Write the number.

Name ______________________________

Night Sky
Develop Concepts

Use with *ScienceFusion* pages 99–102.

day night

DIRECTIONS Circle the word that tells when we see stars in the sky.

Sum It Up!

____

_______ stars

DIRECTIONS James counted stars in the sky. Circle sets of ten stars. Count the sets of stars by tens. Write how many.

Name ____________________

Matter
Develop Concepts

Use with *ScienceFusion* pages 23–26.

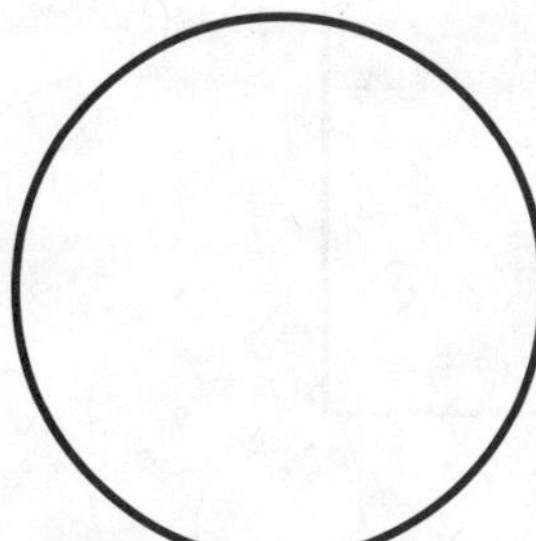

DIRECTIONS 1. Draw an object that is shaped like a square. 2. Draw an object that is shaped like a circle.

Develop Concepts

DIRECTIONS **3.** Find which shapes are the same. Color all the shapes that are the same one color. Use as many colors as the types of shapes.

Name ________________________________

Solving Problems

Develop Concepts

Use with *ScienceFusion* pages 13–16.

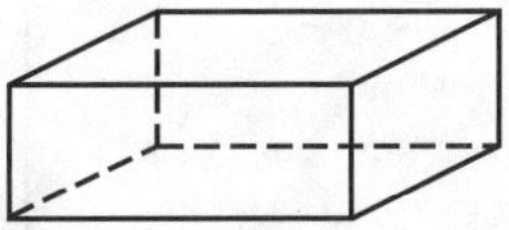 [rectangular prism]	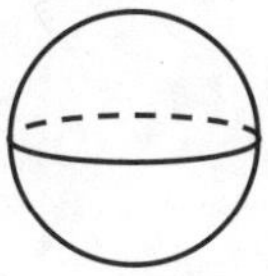 [sphere]	 [cylinder]

DIRECTIONS **1.** Find objects that are shaped like the shapes in the chart. In each column, draw to show the things you found.

Sum It Up!

	Does it roll?	Does it stack?	Does it slide?

3

DIRECTIONS **2.** Look at the shape at the beginning of each row. Decide if it can roll, stack, or slide. Mark an X or insert a check mark in each space to tell if that shape can roll, stack, or slide. **3.** Draw to show an object that rolls and does not stack.

Name ______________________________

Light

Develop Concepts

Use with *ScienceFusion* pages 33–36.

Morning

Afternoon

Evening

2

DIRECTIONS **1.** Look at the pictures. Circle one time of day.
2. Draw to show something you do at that time of the day.

Sum It Up!

Morning

Afternoon

Evening

DIRECTIONS **3.** Draw a line from the time of day to the shadow it may cause on the tree.

Name ______________________________

Using Magnets
Develop Concepts

Use with *ScienceFusion* pages 61–62.

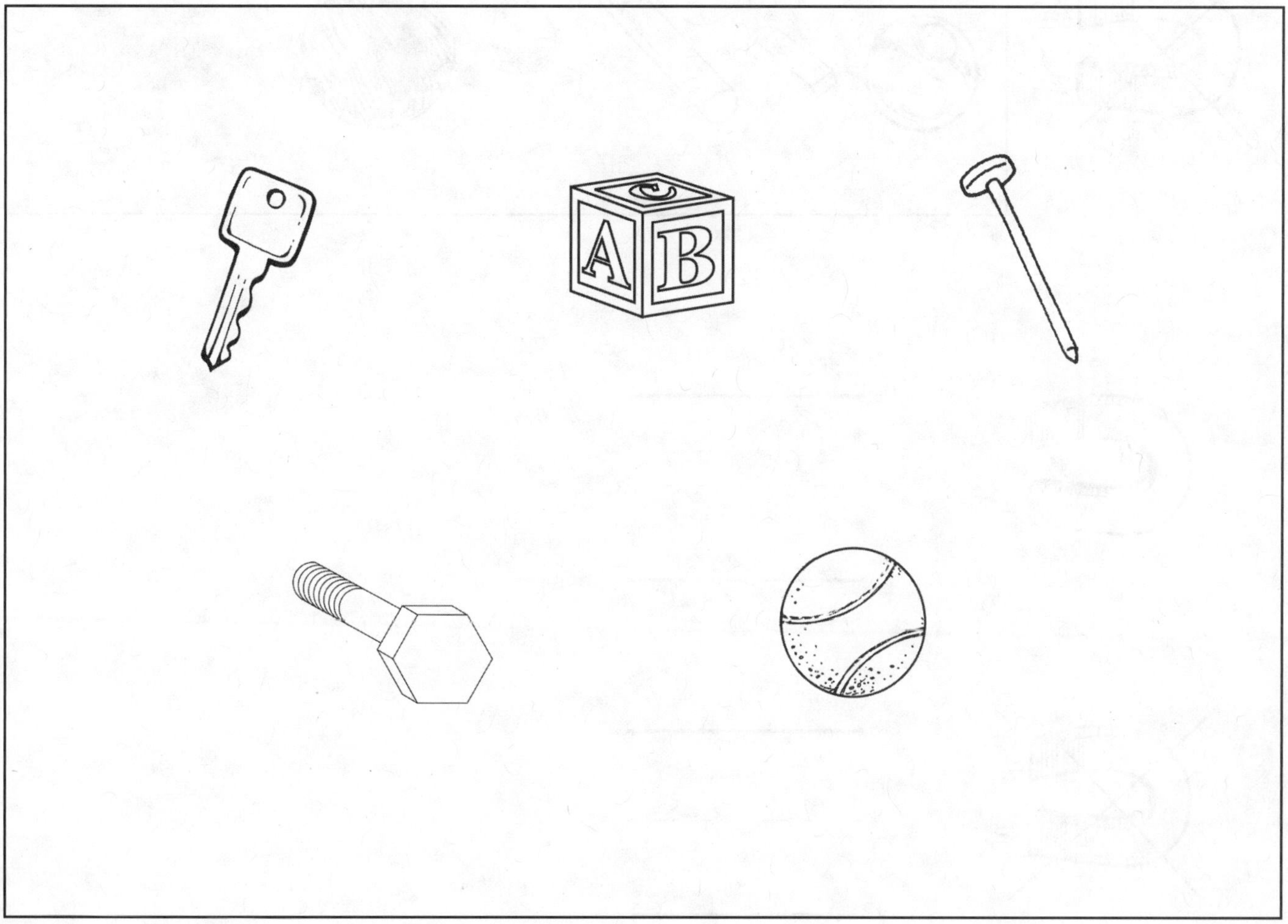

DIRECTIONS 1. Decide which objects the magnet will attract. Circle the objects the magnet will attract. Mark an X on objects the magnet will not attract.

Sum It Up!

	Magnets

2. 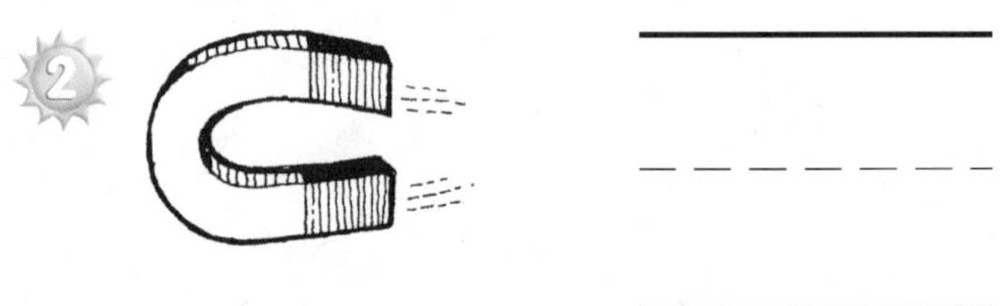

3. 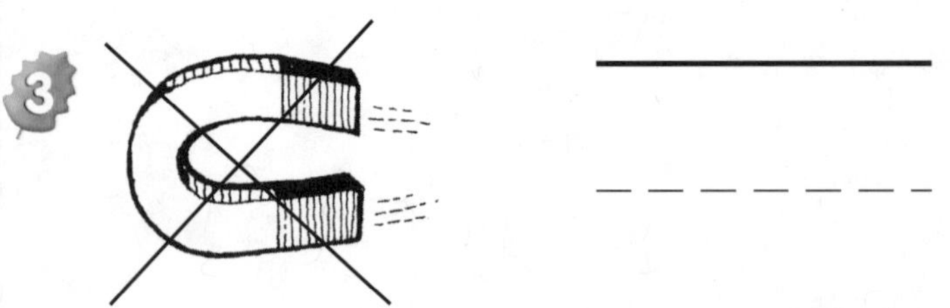

DIRECTIONS Look at the graph. **2.** How many objects does the magnet attract? Write the number. **3.** How many objects does the magnet not attract? Write the number.